Lindis=Chloe Guinness

NUREYEV

Books by Clive Barnes:

BALLET IN BRITAIN SINCE THE WAR
FREDERICK ASHTON AND HIS BALLETS
DANCE SCENE U.S.A. (PHOTOGRAPHS BY JACK MITCHELL)
INSIDE AMERICAN BALLET THEATRE
BEST AMERICAN PLAYS, SERIES SIX AND SEVEN (ED.)
NUREYEV

Books under the Imprint:
A Helene Obolensky Enterprises, Inc. Book

THE BOLSHOI BALLET (PHOTOGRAPHS BY JUDY CAMERON)
INSIDE AMERICAN BALLET THEATRE by Clive Barnes
AMERICA DANCES by Agnes de Mille
NUREYEV by Clive Barnes

NUREYEV
BY CLIVE BARNES

A HELENE OBOLENSKY ENTERPRISES, INC. BOOK
HELENE OBOLENSKY ENTERPRISES, INC.
1982

Grateful acknowledgments are given to the respective sources for the use by the author of his earlier text material, as excerpted or in quotations:

From the New York Times Company © 1964/65/66/67/68/69/70/71/72/73/74/75/76/77. Reprinted by permission.

For "material extracted from the Times of London between 1961 and 1965, copyright of Times Newspapers Ltd." By permission of the Times of London.

For "some of the material which originally appeared in the *Spectator* (London) between 1961 and 1965." Reproduced by permission of the Editor.

Acknowledgment of copyrighted material for photographs is made to the following: Ken Bell © Agence Bernand, © Agence France Presse - Pictorial Parade, © Camera Press Ltd. (Delmas, Reg Wilson), © Judy Cameron, © Central Press, © Susan Cook, © Anthony Crickmay, The Dance Collection at the New York Public Library, Lincoln Center, Astor, Lenox and Tilden Foundations, © Mike Davis Studios, Ltd., Lila Diamond, © Zoë Dominic, Erik Dzenis, © Fredrick Eberstadt, © R. Faligant, © Beverley Gallegos, © Gamma (CBS, Fornaciari, Francolon, Giribaldi, Mali, Schreiber-UDO), © Lois Greenfield, © Henry Grossman, © Walter Healy, Jean Luce Huré, Tana Kaleya, © Keystone Press Agency Inc., © Liaison (Botti), © Serge Lido, © Magnum Photos (Elliott Erwitt), Dina Makarova, © Colette Masson, © Jack Mitchell, J. Oghidanian, © André Ostier, © Paris-Match (Garofalo, Gérard, Letac), © Louis Péres, © Roger Pic, © Pitre Agency Photo Press, William J. Reilly, © Roy Round, © Arks Smith, © Leslie E. Spatt, © Theatre Museum © Houston Rogers Collection, (Victoria and Albert Museum, London), Enid Theobald, Valentino © 1977. United Artists Corporation. All rights reserved., © United Press International, © Monique Valentino (Botti), © Jack Vartoogian, © Linda Vartoogian, Georgina Villacorte, © Jürgen Vollmer, © Wide World Photos,, G.B.L. Wilson, © Reg Wilson, © Rosemary Winckley.

DESIGN BY BEVERLEY VAWTER GALLEGOS

Library of Congress Catalog Card Number 82-145-45
ISBN 0-9609736-2-1

Helene Obolensky Enterprises, Inc.
P.O. Box 87 909 Third Avenue
New York, N.Y. 10150

Printed in the United States of America
First Edition

To Trish

for her help, support and enthusiasm

ACKNOWLEDGMENTS

Despite her wish to remain anonymous, our grateful thanks go to Elaine Rawlings, as her selfless dedication, meticulous research, expert editing, and unfailing devotion have been invaluable to the project.

Sincere thanks and appreciation to Jane Wilson for her kind support and most efficient assistance.

Special heartfelt thanks to Beverley Gallegos for her judicious help and tasteful designs.

Grateful acknowledgment and deep indebtedness to Robert Gable for providing access to and the use of his magnificent private collection.

Further thanks to the Royal Ballet Press Office, Patricia Barnes, Beverley Gallegos, Serge Lifar, Elaine Rawlings, Arks Smith and Hector Zaraspe for their courtesy in providing selections from their private collections.

Many thanks to the researchers and contributors of illustrations for their patience and cooperation.

For the pertinent quotations from their respective works, the author gratefully acknowledges the following courtesies:

Nureyev, An Autobiography with Pictures by Rudolf Nureyev. Edited by Alexander Bland, Hodder & Staughton Ltd. © 1962 by Opera Mundi.

Autobiography by Margot Fonteyn © 1975, W.H. Allen & Co. Ltd., London, Howard and Wyndham.

Step by Step by Ninette de Valois © 1977, W.H. Allen & Co. Ltd., London, Howard and Wyndham.

John Percival for the London *Times*, 1979 opening review of *Manfred*.

For quotations from his own writings, the author acknowledges the following publications: *Ballet News, Dance and Dancers,* Joffrey Ballet "Homage to Diaghilev" Program, London Festival Ballet Program, *The New York Post.*

CONTENTS

COLOR PLATES

I have never seen any dancer whose movements have so burned themselves on my mind like a brand. I shall recall Nureyev in a series of unforgettable photographs that only my memory took and my heart filtered.

He dances with his mind and his heart.

Clive Barnes

INTRODUCTION

The impact that Nureyev has had on the dance world is more simple to assess than it is to comprehend. He has changed it in a way that is extraordinarily unexpected. Why should one man jumping over a barrier at LeBourget Airport have changed dance history? He is not an impresario such as Serge Diaghilev, who did certainly alter the course of ballet history. He is not a dance innovator in the way that Isadora Duncan was, nor is he even a new style of choreographer such as Michel Fokine. He is not one of those pioneers such as Ninette de Valois or Lincoln Kirstein who managed to build a new ballet company in a culture almost alien to ballet. Nureyev has done none of that.

Everything that Nureyev has done for Western ballet—and he has been crucial in the realization of its image—has derived first and foremost from his dancing. He has become the symbol of the male dancer. While George Balanchine has been announcing to the world that "Dance is Woman," Nureyev has come along to suggest that this is not necessarily true. The initial impact of Nureyev on Western ballet was obviously considerable. He seemed to jump higher than most of us had ever seen anyone jump; he spun with the impersonal intensity of a top; but most of all he projected a special image of a man in a role. At first this was nothing more than the popularity of a great dancer. He had fans, he had adulation, and he had a tidy box-office advance.

That was the moment when Nureyev could have become the Mario Lanza of the dance—not the dance proper, but the dance popular. This he rejected, and he went on to become a new symbol of male dancing.

This was only the beginning. Nureyev transformed the image of male dancing throughout the world—he made it respectable and admired. He also injected all of Western ballet, partly simply by his manic energy, with a new view of Russian dance. It is difficult to explain, but time and time and time again he made Western troupes dance with the individuality of the West and with the traditions of Russian ballet. These things he made happen, and they were enormously important.

IN RUSSIA

Rudolf Nureyev was born on a railway train on March 17, 1938. When I first learned this fact, I admit I could not quite believe it—it seemed so much the classic cliché of the dancer—yet cliché or not, it happens to be true. He was born in the vicinity of Irkutsk, near Mongolia, while his mother and three sisters were journeying to join his father, a soldier stationed in Vladivostok. Both his parents were Tatars. After a certain amount of early wandering—including a retreat from Moscow during the war—when Nureyev was five, his family came to Ufa, a city close to where his father had been born.

Throughout his early days Nureyev had to struggle. Nothing was ever easy. A couple of years after he defected from the Soviet Union, he published an autobiography. Although ghost-written, it caught the spirit of the young Nureyev, and the story it told of privation and determination has never varied, indeed by now has been confirmed by people who knew him in Russia. The picture is that of a loner. His was a difficult childhood, a difficult adolescence, a difficult career. All he knew, it seems, right from the beginning, was that he had to dance, as he told me in an interview in March 1977. This quotation and all subsequent quotations which will appear throughout the text in italics, are part of that same March 1977 interview.

...at the very beginning, as a child at home, I do not dance... There is no question to be best, there is no question to do well or something...just to dance... When one heard on the radio—at certain time of year they play live transmission from Bolshoi, of Nutcracker— *and you heard the music...my tears streamed down my cheeks, and being in a kind of bliss just listening to that music, and thinking "well that could be you."*

...So here you are, sitting two thousand miles away from the Kirov, unable to get there and to study and to be one of them, to join and to dance; this occupied your mind twenty-four hours a day... We considered dancing, mainly associated with the classical form... I did dance those folkloric things and whenever possible I managed to go to two or three different groups just to have chance to dance more and more...

Rudolf Nureyev as a student in the Kirov School (the Vaganova Choreographic Academy), Leningrad, with his teacher, Alexander Pushkin, and with Konstantin Sergeyev, Director of the Kirov Ballet Company. Photograph by Mike Davis Studios, Ltd.

This story of his early life and poverty, his days of training and work with the Kirov, and his escape to the West, has considerable interest. To read it is to understand better Nureyev and his greatness as a dancer.

Even now, years after his mind and body were being formed, those difficulties have left their mark on Nureyev. To a greater extent that most, Nureyev was as much a child of his environment as of his parents.

As a child he knew hunger, privation, crowding, misunderstanding, and a little love. The misunderstanding came first from his father. Hamet Nureyev was, before World War II, attached to the Soviet Army as a political officer. It was his function to teach the troops the basic tenets of Stalinist ideology, and he could not understand why his son never evinced

Photograph courtesy of Arks Smith.

any wish to join the Communist Party. Nureyev could understand why his parents embraced the Party, but its protective bear hug was not for him. He was uninterested in the first place, and distrusted the lack of individuality in the party line in the second.

His father was also strongly opposed to Nureyev's becoming a dancer. He was positive that it was no real career for a person and that all dancers ended up as tramps after their usefulness was expended. In fairness, Hamet Nureyev hardly knew what a dancer was. But then, neither did Rudolf. All that Rudolf knew was that he was happiest when he was dancing, and he joined, enthusiastically, a folk dance troupe.

...There was an instance in Ufa when I took a soloist part...that led to the reality of being possessed by dance to such a degree that nothing for me mattered, not even my

Photograph courtesy of Arks Smith.   15

father's wrath...my determination was greater...he did mention that I should finish school, study...but against those odds, rather heroically, I was battling against him...he submitted to my weakness himself...

Then one wonderful night his mother got a ticket for the ballet at the Ufa Opera. Although it was only one ticket, she managed to sneak in not only Rudolf but his three sisters. The young Rudolf absorbed the atmosphere of the theater as if he were breathing for the first time in his life. He loved the lights, the crystal, the velvet. It was a place of magic, but also intensely a place of magic reality, a place to work, not simply a place to dream. And the performance—his very first ballet, *The Song of the Cranes*—confirmed in fact what he already knew in fancy, repeated to his mind the message of his muscles, and the knowledge of his instinct. He was meant to be a dancer, and not a folk dancer, a ballet dancer. He knew nothing, but felt everything.

He knew that in Ufa he was never going to become a ballet dancer, at least not the kind of ballet dancer he wanted to be. He had to go to Leningrad. He had to work at the Kirov, attend the same school in Rossi Street where generation after generation of Russian dancers had been formed, schooled, and polished. That was as likely as wishing to go to the moon, and—given the times—almost less explicable.

In his autobiography Nureyev puts it very plainly: "From the age of eight I can truthfully say I was possessed. Just as a man consumed by a single passion becomes blind to the rest of the world, so I felt in me the urge, the blind need for dancing and for nothing else." Now in his forties, a man of enormous accomplishment and wide interest, that same blind need that consumed him as a child remains with him. He is still possessed by dancing.

Rudolf's schoolwork was indifferent. His early ambition to learn to play the piano was thwarted—although his love for music, like his need for dance, has never been assuaged— and his life was generally unhappy. Yet there was love, the love of his mother and of his favorite sister, Rosa. There were small pleasures: a coloring book he recalls when he was five, watching trains—a longtime preoccupation—and the joy of movement.

Then there was an early moment of luck. He was taken to a social club in Ufa one day and introduced to an old woman named Udeltsova who had once actually danced in the corps de ballet for Diaghilev and who could tell him something of Anna Pavlova and the Maryinsky days.

I was very lucky, I had that teacher, Udeltsova, who used to be a dancer with the Diaghilev Company. She was from a rich merchant family, so it was at the time not appropriate for them to study at the Maryinsky school. But they were allowed to study privately...and she would tell me how it was with Diaghilev, how it was with Massine,

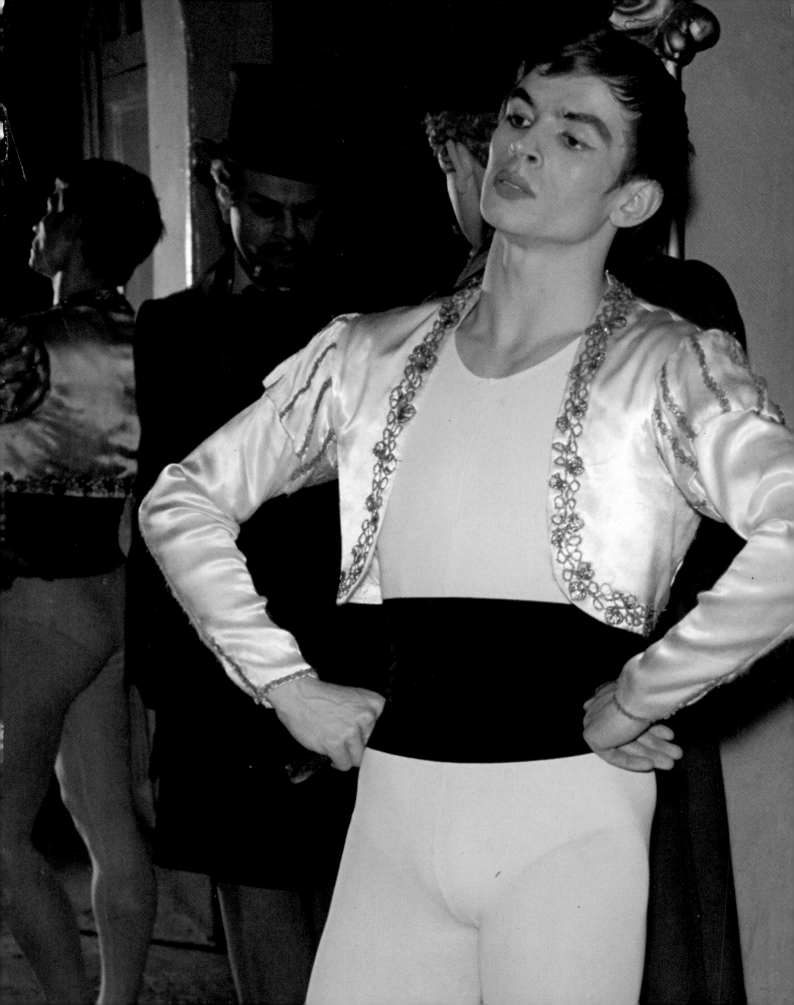

when he came back...I guess he was seventeen when he did that Joseph's Legend...*when Pavlova and Karsavina came from various cities...and when they danced at the Maryinsky ...and how the public was whispering...and then Nijinsky's craze, that was a great scandal blown up by press...that kind of information...I was lucky to have from first hand, for she was* there.

For her Nureyev offered a sort of audition, showing her various folk dances. She was impressed by what she termed his "innate gift" and "his duty to learn classical dancing." She passed him on to a friend of hers, a former Kirov soloist, then teaching in Ufa, named Vaitovich. And it was with her that Nureyev's dance study began in earnest.

He knew—and his new mentors Udeltsova and Vaitovich knew—that he eventually had to get to Leningrad. He yearned for Leningrad as strongly as Chekhov's sisters had yearned for Moscow. But for the present he had to work with Vaitovich. Soon a chance came. A group of children was to be taken from Bashkir, the Soviet Socialist Republic where Nureyev lived, to Leningrad for an audition at the Ballet School. Nureyev desperately wanted to go; but his father could not raise the two hundred ruble train fare. So that first chance was lost.

He continued with his lessons, and he continued with his folk dancing. He even started to give performances, and did walk-ons for the Ufa Ballet at the Opera House.

I used to work as an extra to get to the theater, to be close, to observe, to be close to the ballet, to soak (in) it...on the hope that sometime, suddenly, someone in the corps de ballet would ask me to replace them on five minutes' notice...that was in Ufa...

But his father also maintained his opposition. He would rather have a son who was a good Communist and soldier than a son who was an aspirant dancer and a future tramp. Nureyev persisted.

At one point, so that he could leave day school and make enough money to attend night school, he started to give dance lessons to workers' collectives. Finally a friend helped him to apply to Moscow for a scholarship to the fabled Kirov School in Leningrad. Nothing came of it, but his connections with the Ufa company became stronger and stronger. Eventually he was invited to Moscow to appear with a group of Bashkir artists. He wandered around Moscow, plucked up courage, and contrived an audition with the Bolshoi's greatest teacher, Asaf Messerer. Messerer was obviously impressed and offered the young Nureyev a place in the Bolshoi school.

Common sense would have dictated Nureyev's acceptance of the offer. After all, the Bolshoi was the Bolshoi, and Messerer was a legend. Nureyev described it to himself as "a

miracle." Yet he turned it down. He wanted Leningrad, Rossi Street, and the Kirov School. He was taking a chance.

He knew it. He got the money the Ufa Opera owed him for his appearances in Moscow and bought a ticket for Leningrad. A one-way ticket. He went to the Ballet School, asked to speak to the director, and somehow got accepted for an audition. The audition was before Kostrovitskaya Nureyev tells the story in his autobiography. Kostrovitskaya watched him carefully; then in front of everyone in the classroom announced: "Young man, you'll either become a brilliant dancer, or a total failure. And most likely you'll be a failure."

Now this sybilline utterance sounds almost prophetically glib. Yet the comment was probably smart enough in all conscience. Nureyev was barely trained, and, for the amount of training he had had, no longer especially young. Yet his natural flair, even his looks and physique, and most of all his temperament, marked him out for possible greatness. That kind of potential would rarely be fulfilled even when caught young and diligently nurtured and cossetted. As it was, the teacher must have looked at the gawky faun and admitted,

Rossi Street, Leningrad. Photograph courtesy of Hector Zaraspe.

On Theatre Street (Rossi Street) Photograph courtesy of Arks Smith.

probably with a grim reluctance, that he almost certainly would be "a failure." But surely a failure of the utmost interest, for here was no ordinary possibility. This chrysalis was never going to be a fully-fledged moth. It was destined to be a gorgeous butterfly or absolutely nothing at all.

He was accepted. He had left Moscow for Leningrad on August 17, 1955, at the age of seventeen. Exactly a week later he became a student of the Leningrad Ballet School. He slept in the dormitory, and he joined the school in the Director's own class, the sixth grade—and this in spite of the fact that Messerer had offered him the eighth grade in Moscow! He worked hard at the Kirov, hard at the ballet class and hard at the academic studies, especially those on the histories of art, music, and dance.

He did not do particularly well in the Director's class—the Director was a teacher named Valentin Chelkov. He was also concerned that by being placed in the sixth grade he might be drafted for the Army in the middle of his training. He could hardly risk an interruption after so late a start. He asked to be moved up. Chelkov, not much impressed with him, was amazed. So amazed that he agreed, passing him on to an eighth grade teacher, Alexander Pushkin, at the same time sending Pushkin an unflattering note about the youngster, describing him, possibly with some accuracy, as "an idiot." So Nureyev moved into the class of Pushkin—another piece of luck. Perhaps the most important piece of luck in his entire career.

At first Pushkin paid little attention to the wayward yet serious, brilliant but erratic young Tatar. Slowly he began to see what he had in his studio. Pushkin was one of the most remarkable teachers Soviet ballet has ever produced. I never saw Nureyev in Pushkin's class, but towards the end of the sixties I saw Pushkin teaching many times in Leningrad— when his class included such Kirov dancers as Mikhail Baryshnikov, Valery Panov, and Yuri Soloviev. He was a lovely, loving, careful teacher. His two principal creations as a teacher were, of course, Nureyev and Baryshnikov; two dancers as unlike one another as the two rival Maryinsky ballerinas of the first part of the century—Pavlova and Spessivtseva. Both in their ways are incredible tributes to the man's pedagogic skills. To have produced two such dancers, so different and yet each so exemplary, virtually defines the inspirational nature of Pushkin's teaching.

For Nureyev, Pushkin and his wife became surrogate parents. They welcomed him into their tiny, yet happy, home. Nureyev found someone he could depend on utterly, someone to support him through the tortuous, byzantine political convolutions of the Kirov School and, later, the Kirov Ballet.

He often affects to see deep-laid plots against himself, he will have sudden, gusting feuds with other dancers, he can easily be persuaded that he is being cheated of his rights.

Nowadays such attitudes are often displayed with a tincture of humor, and Nureyev usually is prepared to recognize that the world is not one vast conspiracy pledged to his destruction. But his is not an easy-going personality—and the reason for this undoubtedly stems from his days with the Kirov, days when his position as an outsider seemed to be defined. He seemed to be nobody's favorite.

Generally speaking, he was accepted by the best of his colleagues. When he started to dance with the company—he made his debut with the prima ballerina assoluta Natalia Dudinskaya, no less—the senior ballerina, Alla Shelest, was most helpful and considerate.

With Irina Kolpakova in *Giselle*, Leningrad, 1959. Photograph courtesy of a private collector.   21

22

Among his peers, the late and tragically destined Yuri Soloviev, and the Bolshoi's Vladimir Vasiliev, were consistently friendly and encouraging. But many of the other dancers were mean and envious. Partly, one supposes, this was simple jealousy. The eccentric Tatar boy soon established himself as a firm favorite with the audiences, and was clearly destined for greatness. Yet even jealousy was not the entire story.

Nureyev had always been a solitary runner. He found it difficult to make friends. He was not the slightest bit interested in politics, and he firmly resisted any attempts to recruit him, even nominally, into the Communist Party. Moreover, his very evident and even flaunted individuality could easily be interpreted by the more ideologically-inclined members of the troupe as positively subversive to the Party doctrine. This factor did not make him at all popular with officialdom, which, from the first, seemed to have sensed a dangerously uncontained spirit of rebellion in him. Revolutionaries, of any shape or shade, never seem to be popular in Russia. So, one way or another, the young Nureyev was persecuted. Perhaps he was not persecuted as much as he thought, but he was persecuted all right. Pushkin and his wife were the special barriers for Nureyev between that persecution and total despair. Obsessed with dance, this country boy of naive education yet advanced sensibilities found himself growing up. Even the suddenness of it all took him unawares. Slowly he began to realize his importance, to get a proper assessment of just what he was and how good he was as an artist.

As a dancer everything was going splendidly. As a person and, yes, in the larger sense as an artist, he felt constricted. Bureaucracy looked askance at him. They did not welcome, for example, his courting of foreign artists on the rare occasions when they appeared in Leningrad. To Nureyev such curiosity about the outside world was entirely natural, but to the authorities it revealed non-conformist tendencies and smacked of possible subversiveness. Steps were taken. It was no accident, for example, that when American Ballet Theatre visited Leningrad, Nureyev found himself on a tour of East Germany with a circus troupe! Looking back, just possibly it was an accident, and Nureyev was being too sensitive. But to Nureyev it seemed like a campaign of oppression. Unquestionably, while in the summer of 1961—_that_ summer of 1961—his career was proceeding wonderfully well, he was no company favorite. Many of his colleagues found his flamboyant presence and carefree but careful brilliance a thorn in their foot. As for officialdom, he was considered a troublemaker at best, a man to be watched carefully, certainly not encouraged any more than his talents absolutely demanded. Actually, his talents demanded quite a lot.

In 1956 the Bolshoi Ballet had first visited the West and won an enviable reputation for itself. Soviet ballet, once the big dance question mark hanging over the rest of the dance

Backstage at the Kirov, in costume as Basilio in _Don Quixote_. Photograph by Mike Davis Studios, Ltd.

Overleaf, The Sleeping Beauty at the Kirov Ballet. Nureyev as the Prince, Xenia Ter-Stepanova as Aurora, Oleg Sokolov as the Bluebird, Ludmilla Alexeyeva as Florine, Irina Ultretskaya as the Queen, Yuri Unrekin as Puss in Boots, Galina Kekisheva as the Kitten. Photograph from The Dance Collection, N.Y.P.L.

23

world, was beginning to be appreciated and even understood. It was natural enough that Leningrad's Kirov Ballet, Russia's other great classic troupe, which some thought superior to the Muscovites, should be prepared for overseas visits. The first major tour to the West was planned in the summer, yes, *that* summer of 1961. The company would go first to Paris and then on to London.

When the Bolshoi first appeared in London, and later in New York, it was led by Galina Ulanova, who was already forty-six when she made her Covent Garden debut. By the time the Kirov planned to visit Paris, the company's ballerina, Natalia Dudinskaya, was forty-nine, and her husband and partner, Konstantin Sergeyev, the company's Director, was fifty-one. The Ministry of Culture decided that although the Sergeyevs should lead the company abroad, they should not appear on stage. They were considered too old. Nureyev had not expected to be sent to Paris—he already had been officially informed that his insubordinate behavior in the past would result in his never again being permitted to cross the Soviet border—but under the circumstances, it was decided that Nureyev would go to the West and dance some of Sergeyev's own roles, including the Prince in *The Sleeping Beauty* and Albrecht in *Giselle.* And so he went to Paris.

Serge Lifar presenting the Prix Nijinsky to Nureyev at the Paris Opéra in 1961.
Photograph courtesy of Serge Lifar.

In Boris Fenster's *Taras Bulba*. Photograph by Roger Pic.

As Solor in *La Bayadère*. Photograph by Roger Pic.

30   With Alla Sizova in *The Nutcracker*. Photograph courtesy of Patricia Barnes.

With Ninella Kurgapkina in *Swan Lake*. Photograph courtesy of Patricia Barnes.　31

TO THE WEST

On May 11, 1961 Nureyev said goodbye to Leningrad and flew with the Kirov Ballet to Paris to make his first appearance in the West. On June 17, 1961, at Le Bourget Airport, the young Russian dancer defected to the West and made headlines all over the world. What headlines they were! I have before me the front page of the London *Daily Express* for Saturday, June 17th. There is a huge banner headline across the entire top of the page: "BALLET STAR in drama at Le Bourget. DANCE TO FREEDOM, Girl sees Russians chase her friend." There was even an old picture of Nureyev, dancing in *Don Quixote* at the Kirov, and, of course, for this is the British press, a picture of the girl, Clara Saint. The story itself started: "Russian ballet star Rudolf Nureyev skipped to freedom at a Paris airport today, to the fury of Red security men and the delight of a red-haired girl."

I did not have courage to stay here—just to come and stay—I did not have courage. . .I remember I went to a church, I went to Mary. . .and I said: "make it so that I stay without me doing it, you know, let it happen. . .without me doing it. . .that it will just happen. . . arrange so that I will stay". . .and I did.

During the five weeks that Nureyev had been in Paris, a great deal had happened to him. He did not dance in Paris until May 21st, the fifth night of the company's engagement at the Paris Opéra. Until then, he rehearsed and took class. He also made some new friends, such as Claire Motte and Attilio Labis of the Paris Opéra Ballet, and he explored Paris. This was unusual enough.

In those first days of Soviet touring, the dancers were herded together as a collective. They did everything together—they danced together, they ate together, they went sight-seeing together, they went to receptions together. All this hardly had to be imposed, for such behavior comes absolutely naturally to most Soviets. They expect to be treated in this way, and they even welcome such treatment. Discipline and conformity are all part of the Soviet system. Nureyev was always a rebel—once he even got lost sightseeing in Kiev and missed a

Photograph by Elliott Erwitt/Magnum Photos.

33

train. In Paris he went off on his own—despite all pleadings to the contrary. Nureyev was clearly making his own rules.

The Kirov Ballet at that time was a most unusually gifted troupe. Its repertory was interesting, its style impeccable, and it had a group of new dancers on the eve of shattering the world. True the senior dancers, Dudinskaya and Sergeyev, were not dancing (in London an audience petition for them to give at least *one* performance at Covent Garden, while much appreciated by the veteran dancers themselves, was to no avail), but the troupe was full of talent. There were Yuri Soloviev, Alla Sizova, and Natalia Makarova, three brilliant youngsters at the beginning of their careers. Then there were rather more senior dancers, such as Irina Kolpakova (today the company's prima ballerina) and her distinguished partner, Vladilen Semyanov, other ballerinas Olga Moyeseyeva, Irina Zubkovskaya, and Xenia Ter-Stepanova, the character dancers Anatole Gridin and Alexander Pavlovsky, and two men—a little more prominent in London after Nureyev's defection than they had been in Paris—Oleg Sokolov and Serge Vikulov.

By any standards this was a great company, a company full of promise. The sensation was Nureyev, and with his new celebrity and his mixing with the Western world, the dangers must have been evident to the Soviet authorities. They therefore took what they felt to be the appropriate steps.

While the company was waiting to board a British Airways flight to London, Nureyev was unexpectedly informed that he was to return to Moscow to give a performance at the Kremlin. He would, he was assured, rejoin the company later in London. Instinctively he did not believe a word of it. He knew, then and there, that once he got on that plane to Moscow he would never be allowed out of the Soviet Union again. To Westerners this may sound fanciful. After all, was it not possible that he really was being invited to dance at a Kremlin gala, and that he was being honored rather than being punished? The speed with which the decision was made—or at least the manner in which the dancer was informed—definitely precluded that. Everyone in the Russian party knew pretty well what Nureyev's urgent summons really meant. This was a familiar Soviet tactic. Two years earlier a dancer from Leningrad's Maly Ballet (another non-conformist, Valery Panov, who was later to join the Kirov itself and make headlines as a Jewish dissident) had been sent home from concert appearances in New York on a trumped-up excuse and not permitted to leave Russia again. (Eventually in 1974 Panov and his wife Galina were allowed to leave Russia. Ironically in 1980, Nureyev had one of his most dramatic triumphs playing the epileptic Prince Myshkin in Panov's staging of Dostoievsky's *The Idiot* for the Berlin Ballet.) Nureyev then had had little time to choose his future. Luckily he needed little time.

Backstage at the de Cuevas Ballet, June, 1961, Paris. The first press conference after Nureyev's defection. Photograph by Serge Lido.

35

The company left without him. He got a phone call through to Clara Saint, the Chilean girl who had befriended him in Paris. She came to the airport and alerted the French police. There were still Soviet security guards watching him. He asked for the protection of the French authorities. Despite the protests of the Russians, Nureyev was taken into French hands, and then for a brief time he was placed in a solitary room to think things over. He made his move. What he wrote in that early autobiography is revealing. "Then," he says, "there was silence. I was alone. Four white walls and two doors. Two exits to two different lives." One door led back to a hall where he could proceed to catch the plane waiting to take him to Moscow, while the other would leave him with the French officials and set in motion his defection to the West. He says: "For me this was already a return to dignity—the right to choose, the right I cherish most of all, that of self-determination."

His choice was never in much doubt, but even so, one wonders what thoughts and fears criss-crossed his mind at that moment. Few of us have our decisions so neatly laid out for us; few have such clear-cut choices. Nureyev had not left Russia intending never to return. His defection was forced upon him and was in no way a political act. He felt—and surely rightly—that if he were to fulfill completely his need to dance, he had to leave Russia.

In those eleven years of waiting to get to Kirov school—of course you travel in your mind, and with the help of a map, to all the places so far you knew the existence of, Paris, Milano, London, the Metropolitan, Buenos Aires...and you knew the importance of all those places as being centers of ballet...

The Western world he was entering was no picnic either. In a curious way he had a job waiting, although nothing of the sort had been planned. In Paris he had met Raymundo de Larrain. A friend of the Marquis de Cuevas, who had just died, he was then the Director of the de Cuevas Ballet. This large French-based company had recently staged a new production by Bronislava Nijinska and Robert Helpmann of *The Sleeping Beauty*. Almost immediately after his defection Nureyev had a contract—a six-month contract—with the de Cuevas Ballet and was dancing in Paris two of the same roles he had appeared in with the Kirov, the Prince and the Bluebird in *The Sleeping Beauty*. He made his debut with the de Cuevas company on Friday, June 23rd, partnering one of France's greatest ballerinas, Nina Vyroubova. The prologue to his career was over. Nureyev was a citizen of the world, or at least the Western world. For he had, let it never be forgotten, cut himself off from part of his birthright.

Pressure was instantly placed upon him to return to Soviet Russia. Telephone calls and messages came from his mother, his father, his sister Rosa, and even the Pushkins. Nureyev

Rehearsing the Bluebird pas de deux for the de Cuevas production of *The Sleeping Beauty*.   37
Photograph by Roger Pic.

remained adamant, though the Soviet authorities never ceased their attempts to persuade him to return home. Even years after the defection, the veteran Bolshoi dancer Gyorgy Farmanyants, in London with a troupe of Soviet Army dancers, was commissioned by the Russians to make yet another attempt to persuade the prodigal son to return. Nureyev never accepted the offers or believed the assurances of forgiveness. After all, for him, or any other defector, to be forgiven would have set a precedent no police state could live with.

When Nureyev first arrived in the West, he was both skeptical and adoring. He probably still is. Like many Russians who feel cut off from the mainstreams of art and can recognize the obvious limitations of propagandist output overlain with bureaucracy, Nureyev from his earliest dreams was enormously drawn to the West. He envisaged this a parade of palaces, a meeting of minds, and a place where the artist was free and flourishing. It was a romantic view, but one shared by many. Perhaps one could compare it with the

In Geneva, August, 1961. Photographs by Gery Gérard/Paris Match.

view Germany—represented by men such as Bertolt Brecht, Kurt Weill, and Franz Kafka—took of the United States after World War I. Totally fanciful, and yet with a fancy that through the unknown took on its own dimensions of reality. Nureyev imagined that Western ballet would be superb—a dream of excellence. That was the adoring part. But then he discovered that the standards of schooling, at times even of presentation, were rather less in the West than in the Russia he had left. That was the skeptical part.

Nureyev knew very little about the Western world and very little about Western ballet. Also, like every Soviet refugee settling in the West, he was gloriously unprepared for the demands of our contemporary civilization. The Soviet citizen is brought up to expect the State to have a paternalistic regard for him. Everything is planned from birth to death by an all-seeing and, largely, comfortable bureaucracy. This is no place for political ideology, but unquestionably people brought up in the coarse feather bedding of the Soviet system, even though they may have sufficient spirit to rebel against it, are nevertheless initially nonplussed when faced with Western free enterprise.

They quickly learn that one of the first Western freedoms offered is the freedom to fail, even, possibly, the freedom to starve. Nureyev never really had any economic problem. There was never any question of his being able to make his own living and, more importantly for a refugee, to do in the West what he had done in his homeland, and at more or less the same level of repute and achievement.

He did have a few surprises about Western ballet and the Western art scene in general. He was soon to discover, for example, the Western dance companies were not, by and large, financially so well-endowed as their Russian counterparts. There was freedom of expression, but there could be commercial taskmasters, expressed through the need for box-office success, almost as taxing as those of the Soviet State. But very different.

Well... Gosh... coming from Russia, where everything is centralized... I remember I thought centralization of all those modern companies together, was greatly the answer—because they are all struggling... Seeing Paul Taylor struggle... why couldn't they be under one theater, under one permanent umbrella?... Then, later I thought, well, then there will be head of the whole thing who will impose one style, and everything... So the search in modern-dance will terminate, like in Russia, and this creative germ will be killed... So the corps de ballet really should be a jungle, leaving the jungle as it is, where the strongest survive and those with talent—I always maintain that if they do have talent—they never disappear...

There was, as Nureyev instantly discovered, far more "self-determination" of the kind he needed. Yet the dance world in particular was not serious as it was in Russia. The companies, for the most part, did not have the same traditions. Nureyev soon formed the opinion that a man was as good as he was paid, that in the Western art world there was a price tag on everything and everyone, and the greater the artist the higher his price. It was a cynical but hardly an unrealistic philosophy. He was also soon disillusioned by the quality of Western ballet companies. He looked at the de Cuevas company, for example, and perceived a few good dancers but little discipline, little taste, and a great deal of mediocrity. Audiences, particularly Parisian audiences at that time, did not seem to care.

Then there was the press to contend with. For any Soviet refugee settling in the West, the freedom of the press is quite difficult to handle. For an artist, it can be extraordinarily painful. Nureyev first experienced Western criticism when he danced with the Kirov in Paris. Columns of uninformed ecstasy gushed over him. And, to his surprise, he discovered that not only could anyone express a critical opinion in print, but quite frequently such opinions were woefully uninformed and even partisan. Moreover, what the French press really found interesting about the Russian firebird or Soviet sputnik (it was the beginning of Soviet space exploration, hence the sobriquet) in their midst was not how he danced, but how he had come to them and, strangest of all, the most intimate details of his private life. For Nureyev was not merely introduced somewhat suddenly to the Western ballet critic, he also made acquaintanceship with that other figure—even more bizarre to Soviet eyes—the Western gossip columnist.

Life was not easy. Soon after his defection he found himself in a German television studio for the first time. He was to dance in *Giselle* and in Fokine's *Le Spectre de la Rose* in a program arranged by the Swiss balletmaster Vaslav Orlikovsky, partnering Yvette Chauviré. He was not told what to do, he was expected to *know* the Fokine choreography, which he had never seen. He studied a few photographs of Nijinsky and, with a little help from a few friends, improvised and hoped for the best. His opinion of Western ballet was hardly enhanced, nor was he enamoured of our television studios.

When he defected, I had the pleasure and responsibility of conducting his first TV interview in English. I had met him only to smile briefly at a welcoming reception; but here he was, speaking comparatively little English, looking something like an exotic caged animal, and all in front of BBC cameras. It could have been worse—nothing caught on fire and no one was killed—but not much. The interview took place in an old ballet studio. Outside it seemed to me that there was an undue amount of traffic noise while we were recording; but I was far too inexperienced to question a sound engineer. After the interview—which had gone very interestingly—that same sound engineer announced that there was too much traffic noise, but that the interview had seemed to be going so well that he did not want to

In Geneva. Photograph by Gery Gérard/Paris Match. 41

stop and that we could repeat the whole thing later. Nureyev, knowing a rat when he smelled one, picked up his bag (which I am reliably informed was full of cash, because at that time he did not trust banks) and rushed out into the night.

Nureyev is totally professional—always has been probably from birth. He knew the value of publicity in the West—even though he hated that value. So he came back the next day, and we sort of repeated the interview. It wasn't at all the same. It lacked the spark of the original encounter, but it more or less worked. And the sound quality was exquisite.

We talked of why he had left Russia—he stressed even then that it was non-political—a desire for more artistic freedom. "My leaving Russia was purely artistic and not political. I am not a political person. As I was never a member of the Communist party, I could hardly have left it. But artistically I have found more personal freedom in the West."

I never missed a performance of Dudinskaya or Alla Shelest ... I was always there... Male dancing was very rough in Russia at the time: they did not believe in lyrical passages, they did not believe that man could execute woman's steps, and that's what I was doing. They could not believe it, they could not be emotional; they could not really find that negative feeling which men are never permitted there; it was always positive...

We talked about Russian training methods, the influence of Stanislavsky on the Russian dance as well as on the Russian theater, and what, naturally, he, Nureyev, wanted to do in the West. It was then that he pointed out that he was "a Romantic dancer." I skimmed over it at the time. What did this mean? That he wanted to dance Albrecht in *Giselle* or Siegfried in *Swan Lake*, or all those other cardboard heroes? Couldn't he have done this in Russia? Well, I was clearly wrong. I think Nureyev was trying to express his conception of the role of the dancer as an artist—and he sees that in very isolated, remote, and, yes, romantic terms. There will always be a kind of broodingly Byronic quality of flamboyant reserve to Nureyev's view of the artist. He is religious in his dedication to his art, also irreverent about it in the way only the devout can be. But he needs to put a fence around his soul, if not his heart.

...in their mood, it is not there...their souls...they do not travel...

And this indeed would be a Romantic dancer. Brooding and aloof, Nureyev is the epitome of the Romantic ballet hero. Here is the Romantic dancer of our century, a dancer whom even Nijinsky's partner, Karsavina, thought to be Nijinsky's peer if not superior.

What is Nureyev really like? One wonders whether even Nureyev knows. Although often full of a manic happiness, and usually an enchanting person to be with, he is withdrawn, or at least a part of him is withdrawn. He lives a double life and works hard at it. Most people elevated to super-stardom by the special needs of our society decide to give up a private life. Rudolf Nureyev has never done that. He has very private friends, some famous, some unknown; and he lives for his work, not the peripheral fame and glamour that work has brought him.

It is amazing how much Nureyev knows—about plays, films, novels, politics, almost any human activity you can think of, he has information on a high level of concern. Curiously, I have never heard him mention sports—that is perhaps the one thing he has not found time for. It is equally amazing how much of his conversation—at least with me, who admittedly may not be typical of his acquaintanceship—is concerned with dance, even the minutiae of dance, even the gossip of dance.

Dance has engulfed Nureyev, but he still floats on it. He is by no means the kind of dancer who thinks and dreams of nothing else. He experiences an enormous number of things, private, public, and artistic, but it seems that—rightly so—they all feed his art. You wouldn't think of discussing the latest Robert Altman movie with George Balanchine, or wondering with Margot Fonteyn where the avant-guardist Robert Wilson was going. But with Nureyev such things are important. Generally speaking, he likes to listen rather than talk, but when he talks, it is with the devastating sense of a natural logician. He has a great eye and ear for the pretentious. He is wary. He has an odd, ironic wit that is absolutely delightful. I recall from that first TV interview asking the natural, dumb, obligatory TV question: "How do you feel being compared with Nijinsky?" Nureyev smiled a Tatar smile and replied with a tone dripping with honey: "Well, of course it's flattering;" and then with a glint of naughty irony, "but I feel sorry for Nijinsky—for him it cannot be so flattering." And that was after he had been in England for a total of about ten days.

He is an impulsive man. He will suddenly appear unannounced at friends' doors. Then he will sit down, almost without speaking, leaf through magazines for a time, and slide away just as quickly as he arrived. He can be rowdy, he can be quiet. In this, one supposes, he is very Russian—the life and soul of the party, but always with a lingering Slav melancholy.

He is a man of great personal loyalties, enormous generosity, and the occasional artistic feud (the currently healed, much publicized battle with Natalia Makarova, for instance) that seems like a mixture of concern, jealousy, and despair. Remember that the Romantic artist is searching for an ideal—in Nureyev's case it is the quest for artistic perfection, creative inspiration, and career permanence. For a short order cook that would be a long order—for a dancer it is impossible, but very Romantic.

During the early months of his defection, three colleagues were particularly helpful to Nureyev—the Franco-American ballerina, Rosella Hightower, the Bulgarian-born British ballerina, Sonia Arova, and that international Dane, Erik Bruhn, who was the reigning male dancer of his day. Nureyev danced with the ballerinas and was befriended by Bruhn, the man he felt could teach him more about dancing than anyone else in the world. When his contract with the de Cuevas company expired, Nureyev went to Copenhagen to stay with Bruhn, who was on one of his comparatively rare visits to his homeland, and to study with the supreme Western teacher, a sometime pupil of Agrippina Vaganova, Vera Volkova.

Volkova was then the balletmistress to the Royal Danish Ballet. Previously she had been associated with Britain's Royal Ballet, and her most celebrated pupil was Margot

Quartet rehearsing: Nureyev, Sonia Arova, Erik Bruhn and Rosella Hightower. Photograph by Serge Lido.

On the French Riviera, rehearsing with Rosella Hightower. Photograph by Delmas/Camera Press Ltd. 45

Curtain call for the quartet: Rosella Hightower, Sonia Arova, Erik Bruhn, and Nureyev. 1962.
Photograph by Garofalo/Paris Match.

In a performance of *Fantaisie* with Rosella Hightower. Photograph: Roger Pic.   47

Fonteyn, who was to become Britain's prima ballerina assoluta. It was while Nureyev was with Volkova that the telephone rang and the teacher passed it over to him, saying "It's for you." It was Fonteyn.

Fonteyn had, for some years, been President of Britain's Royal Academy of Dance, an organization that was chronically hard up. It was in 1958 that Fonteyn came up with the bright idea of holding an annual fund-raising gala. In 1961 this was to be held on the afternoon of November 2nd at the Theatre Royal, Drury Lane. Fonteyn had originally hoped to get Galina Ulanova as her star, but Ulanova regretfully had had to withdraw. Fonteyn was advised that Nureyev sounded interesting, and he was certainly newsworthy. Their first communications were by telephone. Nureyev wanted to dance with Fonteyn herself, but this was not possible. She was already committed to appear with her long-time partner who had just retired, Michael Somes, and the younger British star, John Gilpin. She could not also dance with Nureyev. A compromise was reached: Nureyev would have a special solo choreographed for him by Frederick Ashton (Nureyev's own request), and he would dance the *Black Swan* pas de deux with Hightower.

Nureyev was first brought to London under a pseudonym. Fonteyn's husband, Roberto Arias, was at the time the Panamanian Ambassador to the Court of St. James; so Nureyev stayed first in London at the Panamanian Embassy. His *nom de guerre*, Roman Jasmin, was adopted to protect him from the press. He even took class at the Royal Ballet School under the pretense that he was a Polish dancer. The pretense did not last long, and he was soon recognized. It was around that time I remember meeting him for the first time at a large reception given at Dame Margot's Embassy in South Kensington. He seemed reserved, self-confident, and rather charming. He also seemed on his best behavior, as doubtless he was.

For that Drury Lane Gala, he pulled out everything he had. The performance was a sensation. Nureyev had always wanted to dance in London even more than in Paris. He had read a great deal about Western ballet and felt, accurately enough, that there was more of an informed public in London than across the Channel. Also he sensed, almost from the beginning, that of all the ballet companies in the Western world, if he was to use one as his base of operations, that one should be Britain's Royal Ballet. Nureyev has always shrewdly understood what was best for his career.

I went along to Drury Lane not knowing at all what to expect—it was the first time I had seen Nureyev dance—accounts of him in class had not been altogether favorable. As this was my first glimpse of the man who was to change Western ballet, it might be worth quoting from my review at the time. It read:

"If at Drury Lane last week Rudolf Nureyev had leapt into the air and dissolved in a

shower of multi-colored sparks, no one would have been disappointed. Nothing less than some such total demonstration could have possibly satisfied the irrational curiosity generated by that escape to the West and that publicity tag of 'the world's greatest male dancer' which dangled around the luckless Russian's neck. He was dancing before an audience ninety-five percent of whom were willing to be 'sent' at the bat of a long eyelash, while the critical remainder sat grimly on their haunches, waiting to be 'shown' and coming out in scandalized goosepimples at the hysteria around them.

"Nureyev was indiscriminately cheered within an inch of his life. For all that, he seems a remarkable dancer. He appeared in two numbers. The first had been newly choreographed by Ashton and looked for the most part little more than a pinchbeck parody of a Soviet-style solo. Set to Scriabin's *Poème Tragique* (apparently Nureyev's own choice), this mixture of sobs and spins, a technical display with an unrelated obbligato of anguished hair-tearing, had a startling undertone of symbolism. At the rise of the curtain, Nureyev was discovered against the backcloth, draped in an enfolding red cloak. He struggled off with the cloak, threw it down, hurtled towards the footlights (westward), stopped, and then gazed at the audience with the agony of a stricken faun. It was a moment of deplorable taste and thrilling theater. This face of pain, crumpled into tragedy, the tense body held in an animal pose of fright, too obviously seemed to exploit his personal plight. But nothing else he did so manifestly showed his potential capabilities as this blatant, piercing moment of communication.

"Technically, Nureyev is excellent, though by the standards of his peers (say Soloviev or Bruhn), he is somewhat untidy around the feet. He has a great deal of nervous energy, as opposed to stamina, and his dancing sputters rather than burns. His arms lack masculinity, being softly graceful, but—and this is important—more in the way of an immature boy than an effeminate man. The result is oddly sexless, which is perhaps where the oft-made comparison with Nijinsky has arisen. Of all the dancers docketed as 'the New Nijinsky,' Nureyev is the first in my experience to resemble remotely any of the famous descriptions of him.

"He dances with some arrogance, and often a certain sardonic half-smile flickers over his face. His personality seems elusive and changes quickly—now he is the favorite child showing off in front of his neighbors, now the Tatar warrior come down from the hills, now the great romantic hero swooping up hearts like a Valentino eagle. In the *Black Swan* pas de deux, the second of his two appearances, he proved less interesting than in the intrinsically tawdry Scriabin. Here and there were glints of the real Siegfried, doused by a long blonde wig which gave him a ridiculously epicene air; too often his boyish charm wilfully obscured his deeper gifts. At times he appeared to be challenging the audience to cheer the circus they had paid for, cynically cracking his body like a ringmaster's whip. After he had encored his

exhausting solo, fighting his way through his final and by now erratic double air-turns, he looked like a blissfully successful martyr. A fascinating dancer of whom we have neither seen the last nor the best. He should be invited to make his career with the Royal Ballet."

Not unexpectedly, I was hardly the only member of the audience of that last opinion about Nureyev's future. It was shared, happily enough, by Dame Ninette de Valois, the Director of the Royal Ballet. And the acquisition of Rudolf Nureyev was to be her final, and in some ways, most brilliant coup before she retired.

It was not actually his dancing that first attracted her. As she has written in her collection of essays, *Step by Step*, it was Nureyev's curtain calls that won her over: "I saw an arm raised with a noble dignity, a hand expressively extended with that restrained discipline

In *Poème Tragique*, the first work choreographed especially for Nureyev by Frederick Ashton, at Dame Margot Fonteyn's Gala Matinee for the Royal Academy of Dance at the Theatre Royal, Drury Lane on November 2, 1961.

Rehearsing *Poème Tragique*. Photographs from the Theatre Museum, Houston Rogers Collection
(Victoria and Albert Museum, London).

which is the product of a great traditional schooling...I could see him suddenly and clearly in one role—Albrecht in *Giselle.* There and then I decided that when he first danced for us it must be with Fonteyn in that ballet." Naturally enough it was.

Fonteyn herself needed a little persuading. At the time of Nureyev's London debut, Fonteyn was already forty-two years old. She was not exactly thinking of retiring—the days when she had announced that she would retire when she reached thirty were fortunately well behind her. After all Ulanova, whom she had first asked to dance at the Drury Lane Gala, was then nearly fifty-two. Fonteyn's partner for about twelve years, Michael Somes, had decided to withdraw from all but non-dancing parts, and Fonteyn had just taken on a new, younger partner, the twenty-nine-year-old David Blair. When de Valois told Fonteyn that Nureyev was going to dance in *Giselle* the following February and asked whether she would like to dance with him, she said that she would give her answer the following day. That night she discussed it with her husband. They "came to the conclusion that Rudolf was going to be the big sensation of the next year and I had better get on the bandwagon or get out. I called de Valois to thank her for asking me, and accepted," Fonteyn writes in her *Autobiography.* Nureyev was not the only one who arranged his career with shrewdness, nor was de Valois by herself in always eventually getting what she wanted. That partnership made in heaven—Fonteyn and Nureyev—had in its way been skillfully negotiated.

The event took place on February 21, 1962. Between the November Gala and then, Nureyev had been far from inactive. With Bruhn, Hightower, and Arova, he formed a sort of concert group, which rehearsed in Britain and danced in Cannes and Paris, starting in Cannes on January 6, 1962. It gave only four performances in all. On the last performance in Paris, Bruhn injured his foot—and this led to Nureyev's making his American debut on television on *The Bell Telephone Hour* in Bournonville's *Flower Festival* pas de deux, partnering Maria Tallchief.

This first foray in America was, considering the circumstances, surprisingly successful, even though his plane was diverted from New York by a thunderstorm and he first landed on American soil in Chicago.

That first TV shot also led to Nureyev's becoming what was probably ballet's first TV star. It was the great era of the TV Variety Show in the United States—a period when a few performances on the Ed Sullivan Show would later seal the international success of a young English rock group, The Beatles. During his early years in the West, Nureyev danced a great deal on both the Bell Telephone Hour and the Sullivan Show with such partners as Lupe Serrano, Carla Fracci, and Margot Fonteyn.

These quick and dashing displays of pure virtuosity became one of the bases of his fame in North America.

In the Black Swan pas de deux at the Drury Lane Gala, November 2, 1961. Photograph from the Theatre Museum, Houston Rogers Collection (Victoria and Albert Museum, London).

Rehearsing for a television performance with Rosella Hightower. Photograph by Zoë Dominic.

In New York. Photograph: Jack Mitchell.

With Erik Bruhn in a New York studio. Photograph by Jack Mitchell. 57

However, it was his first Covent Garden *Giselle* that February that charted the direction his career was taking. He had, of course, danced Albrecht with the Kirov, he had appeared in the ballet in Paris, and also partnered Yvette Chauviré, one of the greatest Giselles of our time, with the de Cuevas Ballet. But that first *Giselle* with Fonteyn was something different, not simply as performance but as portent.

Fonteyn had never really been totally successful in the ballet. When very young—she first danced the role at age seventeen—she certainly possessed that fragile, youthful poignancy that quite a few young Giselles have, only to lose it with maturity. So it was with Fonteyn—for years *Giselle* had not loomed significantly in her repertory. Yet the Giselle she gave that night with Nureyev was different—more deeply felt, more rhapsodic, more intense. It was the first indication, and it seemed almost incredible, that Fonteyn's career could take on, even at that apparently late stage, a new lease with her new young Russian partner.

As Albrecht in his first London performance in *Giselle.* February 21, 1962, Royal Ballet, Covent Garden. Photograph by Roy Round.

Rehearsing *Giselle* with Margot Fonteyn. Photograph from the Theatre Museum, Houston Rogers Collection (Victoria and Albert Museum, London).

Fred (Frederick Ashton) occasionally came to see Giselle. . . *I remember* Giselle *went very smoothly. . . I remember corps de ballet crying in the second act, during rehearsal, in the studio, just standing there with their tears dripping. . .in the second act. . .and then, at performance, I do not know what happened, I do not remember. . .*

Nureyev, too, showed some of his cards that night. London had previously seen him in only the one brief solo and a somewhat flurried classic pas de deux. In a complete ballet, *Giselle,* he was a revelation. And he clearly went beautifully with Fonteyn. It was evident that something extraordinary was taking place. Right from this very first performance, Nureyev was able to pull a new quality out of Fonteyn: he challenged her. She surpassed herself—brilliantly, wonderfully, surprisingly. In a way they were born to dance together.

Yet, thoughtful London critics were disturbed about the cavalier way Nureyev had with the traditional choreography. Nureyev introduced many new things of his own into that *Giselle,* things not only alien to the Royal Ballet production, but choreography that was not to be found in the Kirov version either.

On the other hand, most observers that night were prepared to forgive him virtually anything. They felt they had been present at the beginning of what could be a great partnership—although few, if any, that night could have foreseen that they were watching the birth of the most celebrated ballet partnership of the twentieth century, perhaps even of all time.

Interestingly, that night there was one unique event in the curtain calls. In the years to come, Fonteyn and Nureyev were to take the art of the curtain call to new heights, indeed making them an essential coda, almost an encore, of the ballet they had danced. The curtain calls on that first occasion were certainly not so beautifully stylized as they eventually became. However, at the end, Nureyev, carried by the moment and apparently conscious of the significance of the night, swept down on one knee and kissed Fonteyn's hand. By the second performance, they had rehearsed the culminating moment of their calls, which has remained the same throughout their partnership, and this is when Fonteyn curtsies low to Nureyev, gravely presents her hand, which he ceremonially kisses. It is more effective than the impulsive prototype, but it was somehow right that the first performance should have just one unique flourish to it that was never to be repeated.

There was no real question after this that Nureyev would join the Royal Ballet—he was to be called a "guest artist" for it has not been the British company's custom to permit any but British nationals—in those pre-Common Market days taken to include all members of the British Commonwealth—to join the company. But this was a technicality. For the next few years, the Royal Ballet was Nureyev's home and base. The courage, enterprise, and wisdom that de Valois showed in obtaining Nureyev is discussed elsewhere; suffice it here

merely to stress the importance of the Russian to the then still-developing British company, and particularly his effect upon British male dancing. Far from breaking up the happy home, he spurred on a new generation of male dancers and strengthened the Royal Ballet's links with the Russian tradition of Petipa. He was to be a crucial figure in the history of British ballet.

It is his total absorption in a role that provides some of the quality in his dancing. It is this that has led Fonteyn to remark: "When I am dancing with him, and I look across the stage, I do not see Nureyev, a man I know and talk to every day; I see the character of the ballet, for he is absorbed in his role."

Although the Royal Ballet and Covent Garden were to provide Nureyev with a home, he was not going to dance exclusively with any single company. Almost as if to underline that, after the performance of *Giselle* in London, he left for New York, where on March 10th, dancing as a guest artist with Ruth Page's Chicago Company at the Brooklyn

Curtain call after Fonteyn and Nureyev's first *Giselle*. Photograph by G.B.L. Wilson.

Academy of Music, he made his American stage debut. He partnered his friend Sonia Arova in the *Don Quixote* pas de deux. The entire New York dance world, and quite a few more socially inclined, turned up for the debut, which was received a little coolly by critics and dance professionals alike. New York does not give up its skepticism without a fight, and, after all, who did this young Russian think he was, just because he had leapt over an airport barrier? It takes more than that to impress New York.

From now on Nureyev's career was to form into a pattern. His off-stage activities would continue to be newsworthy at a gossip-column level, and indeed Nureyev really did become the first pop star ballet ever had. He truly became a household name, not only for his dancing, although his professional fame always supported his public notoriety. It seemed to be his off-stage antics, either real, exaggerated, or imagined, that caught the fancy of the general public and fanned the flames of his stardom, if the metaphor can be as mixed as the blessing.

It is curious that in this day and age so besotted with the cult of personality, the sort of gossip-column renown that Nureyev had attracted has become a self-fulfilling prophecy. One gets noticed by columnists, in a way, because one is controversial, and one remains controversial because one is noticed; for to be noticed is to be written about, and if people cannot find anything controversial to say about a controversial figure it is their job to invent it. It may have all seemed very puzzling to the boy from Ufa—although I wonder if it really did.

I remember meeting him for a late lunch in a South Kensington cafe in 1964. I was writing a story on him for the *New York Times* Sunday Magazine in preparation for a forthcoming visit by the Royal Ballet to New York. He explained to me that he could not eat, and merely toyed reflectively with a Negroni cocktail—a drink he was at the moment fond of. He had, he said, already had two lunches that day—one with the representative of *Time* Magazine and another with a reporter from *Newsweek*. Both wanted to prepare a cover story on him, and this unsophisticated child of Soviet nature understood immediately that if *Time* did it, *Newsweek* wouldn't, and vice versa. He shrewdly realized that it would be better for all concerned—particularly himself—if each party were kept in ignorance of the other's activities until it became too late. The ploy worked. Nureyev appeared on the covers of both *Time* and *Newsweek* in the same week. Politicians apart, the double cover remains an extreme rarity.

Although he has never employed a publicity man, Nureyev uses the media more brilliantly than most artists ever have. Of course he was, and is, temperamental. Whatever temperamental means. The stories of his slapping ballerinas and throwing plates of food around, while usually having their flowering in a small seed of truth, were almost invariably

With Sonia Arova in *Don Quixote* pas de deux at the Brooklyn Academy of Music, March 10, 1962. Photograph by Jack Mitchell.

exaggerated. In 1965 two prominent magazine stories contained colored accounts of a fracas at a party in Spoleto. In one version Nureyev "threw his wine glass against the wall," in the other "he smashed his whisky glass on the floor." Nureyev himself is vague about the incident, but a friend of mine who was there says: "Rudi happened to drop his glass." The point, of course, is that a legend can never be permitted merely to drop glasses.

Once at a Royal Gala, Nureyev was dancing a solo specially made for him. His shoes troubled him, so he kicked them off and finished barefoot. Probably no other dancer would have done quite that.

He has been known to be horrid to conductors, glaring at them malevolently during curtain calls; and his frankness regarding other dancers, not merely behind their backs, is occasionally less than endearing. But the Nureyev legend is also self-supporting and self-expanding, as indeed all good legends must be.

Through all the vagaries of his temperament runs the steel backbone of his professional discipline. No one in dance works harder. He has genius but he also has common sense to know that he cannot trade on it. He rehearses hours each day, he will argue over lighting cues, he will dance when both feet are strapped up and his doctors are advising caution.

Nureyev has never been an easy man to work with. Legends with temperament probably rarely are.

Even before Nureyev's defection, he had been the talking point of the first Western season the Kirov Ballet had given in Paris. He had the kind of stardom that notoriety might enhance but could never create. Nureyev always seemed good for a paragraph, and the paragraphs added up to a great measure of celebrity.

It was the kind of celebrity that no dancer had ever had before, and it was much helped by the newsworthiness of his partner, Fonteyn. The differences in their ages was interesting copy in itself, and Fonteyn had a habit of getting into the news on her own account. Perhaps her equivalent of the dash at Le Bourget was her participation a short time before Nureyev's defection in an abortive revolution in Panama. Later, and far more tragically, the unsuccessful assassination attempt in Panama on her husband, which left him permanently crippled, was a terrible but attention-grabbing event. If the two of them were famous by themselves, together they were dynamite. Pavlova, for example, was the symbol of a ballet star—the name meant something special to the general public, as Caruso's did as a tenor. Such names passed into the language as a measure of their emblematic acceptance. But Fonteyn and Nureyev soon became actual stars in their own right—stars like Frank Sinatra, Joe Namath, or Brigitte Bardot. They were artists on the one hand and cafe society darlings on the other. They were also very good. Whatever one heard about the outrageousness of

In New York. Photograph by Elliott Erwitt/Magnum Photos.

their behavior (more particularly, his behavior), no one suggested that either as a partnership or individually they did not deliver their promised measure of artistry.

All this time Nureyev was developing, both as a dancer—for when he came westward he was far from maturity—and as a director, choreographer, and general man about ballet. All the time his career was spreading out. His intellectual curiosity was always amazing, and his utter professionalism never less than profound and demanding. His career as a dancer has, in effect, been nothing but a quest for betterment, wherever he might find that.

It has occasionally been suggested—never, I think, by people who know him—that Nureyev came to the West to seek his fortune. This is nonsense. He is reported to be rich, but money is of no importance to him whatsoever, except in one peculiar fashion. As a boy, Nureyev had been taught that capitalism was evil and wealth and its acquisition were wrong, especially if not achieved during the normal course of official Communist Party business. This has left Nureyev with a residual feeling, which was at first strong and has now simply become a habit, that the worth of people in the West, even in a sense the artistic worth, can be measured by how much they earn.

As a result, Nureyev is interested in money merely as a yardstick to his importance. But, everyone in the dance world knows that Nureyev will help out friends by performing virtually for nothing on occasion; and when he is offered something he is particularly anxious to dance, the lack of money is no object. He clearly lives modestly enough.

The actuality of his life came home to me forcibly one night after he had danced at some fund-raising gala. To help the company, he turned up briefly at a white-tie dinner given—if I recall rightly—at the Pierre. Eventually he indicated that he was slipping away, and he asked if my wife and I could join him later at the Navarro Hotel where he was staying. Later we did join him there. The fancy dress of the evening had gone, to be replaced by a blue dressing gown. His feet, in bad shape, were stuck into a bowl of hot water. He was patiently eating a hamburger. So much for the glamour and the life of ease of Rudolf Nureyev.

He works harder than any dancer I know. He is always going to his favorite teachers —teachers such as Valentina Pereyaslavec and Stanley Williams in New York—where each and every day he can be found trying that little bit harder. He says of the former:

. . . when I came to the West, there was. . . Pereyaslavec. . . she created a state of exaltation in the class, it was like prayer in the church. . .

The almost self-flagellating quest for improvement and the desire to involve himself in virtually every branch of dance has led him to become caught on a treadmill of ambition and achievement.

In the studio. Photographs by Fredrick Eberstadt.

As a result of his honorary membership into the ranks of the beautiful people, there are many aspects of his public image which are far removed from his private reality. It is often assumed, to take one example, that Nureyev is a particularly stylish, fashionable, or even natty dresser. Not always. He usually looks slightly modern in his dress, and he is prepared to wear furs and snakeskins that perhaps the more conventional would avoid, but no one could fairly call fashionable a man who tends to wear clothes until they virtually wear out. A couple of jumpsuits designed by Halston, a red leather macintosh, and a fur coat will virtually see him through three or four seasons. He is one of the last men to worry about his appearance.

Then again, thanks to the popular press, he has over the years developed a reputation as a bon vivant, a nightclubber, partygoer, and general sybarite about town. Nothing could be further from the truth. When he eats out, he usually eats nothing but steak and drinks hot sweet tea with lemon. He eats more like an athlete than a gourmet, and he has little time for social chitchat or social niceties. He likes to be lionized, but does not always appreciate being a lion.

The reputation of being rude, wayward, and temperamental, of having tantrums and fits of moodiness have all been greatly exaggerated. There is a depressive side to him. He can sometimes display a manner that is disconcerting to his friends. But he is normally courteous to a fault. Quite definitely he goes through the world expecting that most people will be more interested in him than he will be in them; and this attitude is nothing more than realistic. He does not suffer fools gladly. In fact he does not suffer fools at all—he soon disengages himself, sometimes quite pointedly.

He does not have many close friends, partly because he is difficult to get to know. His years in Russia made him distrustful of people in general and his days in the West as a butterfly-transfixed celebrity, often betrayed, have not done a great deal to increase his simple faith in humanity. However, once he has made friends, he is extremely loyal and trusting. He is also very good company, partly because of the breadth and depth of his interests. It is easy for dancers to lead a sheltered, narrow life that is encompassed almost entirely by the stage and classroom, its achievements, disappointments, and gossip. Nureyev does his share of gossiping and, more importantly, thinking narrowly and minutely on the minuscule details of his craft, as well as their larger implications. While he is obsessed with dance, no one could accuse him of being simply obsessed with dancers and dancing.

Her Majesty Queen Elizabeth II with Fonteyn and Nureyev after a performance of Pelleas et Mélisande at Covent Garden on the occasion of Dame Margot's 35th anniversary at the Royal Ballet, March 29, 1969.

Their Royal Highnesses Prince Charles and Princess Anne after a Gala performance of Nureyev's production of The Nutcracker, February, 1968, Royal Opera House, Covent Garden.

Escorting H.R.H. Princess Margaret to a reception at the Royal Academy of Dance, London, March, 1968. Dame Margot Fonteyn in the background.

Photographs by Keystone Press Agency, Inc.

I remember, for example, he was once curious about a new production of Lorca's *Yerma,* which made use of trampolines and had become a theatrical sensation in Europe. It was playing at the Brooklyn Academy of Music when Nureyev was in the course of a North American tour. He made the most strenuous efforts to arrange his schedule to get back to see this *Yerma.* All to no avail. *Yerma* and Nureyev just could not be brought together. Undaunted, he asked a friend to sit in the top gallery and film the performance with a silent hand-held camera to give him some idea of the technique involved.

This anxiety to keep abreast of the general world of performing arts was typified for me a few years ago when Robert Wilson (another avant-garde theater figure admired by Nureyev) was also appearing in Brooklyn. Halfway through the performance, Nureyev quietly slipped in. He had come in from Europe that afternoon and had already been taking class and rehearsing with Martha Graham. He had come over to Brooklyn on the off chance, because he knew Wilson was playing. Seeing him afterwards, my wife invited him home for a simple steak. He agreed and on the way in the cab he asked about Robert Altman's movie *Nashville* which he had yet to see. He noticed in the paper that a performance was just starting, and he instantly decided to see it on the way to supper. We, who had already seen the movie, continued on home, and he followed on about three hours later. We talked until the morning hours, then he went off and was at ballet class that same morning. This is Nureyev with jet lag.

With Carla Fracci. Photograph by Keystone Press Agency, Inc.

With Natalia Makarova at Maxim's, Paris, 1977. Photograph by Letac/Paris Match.

With Julie Andrews. Photograph by Zoë Dominic.

With Zizi Jeanmaire. Photograph by Roger Pic.

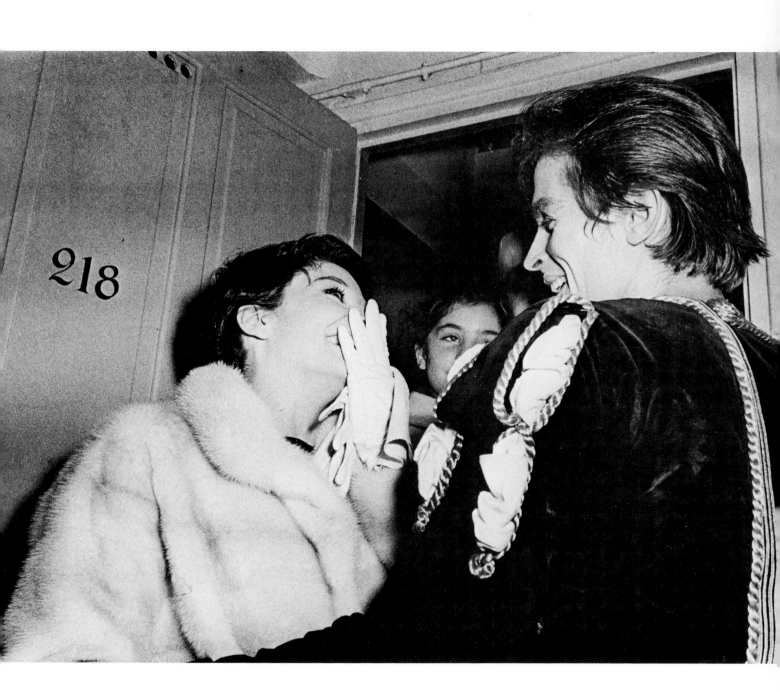

74   Above, left, with Pierre Bergé of Maison St. Laurent, President of the Chambre Syndicale of the French Couture; Philippe Grumbach of *l'Express*; and Jean Marais. At Maxim's, Paris, 1981. Photograph by Jean-Luce Huré. Above, right, with Antoinette Sibley in Monaco, 1973. Photograph by Gilbert Giribaldi/Gamma. Below, left, with Maestro Leopold Stokowski. Photograph by United Press International. Below, right, with Maria Callas, Roland Petit, and Margot Fonteyn, 1967. Photograph by André Ostier.

Above, Maurice Chevalier greeting Margot Fonteyn and Nureyev after a performance of *Swan Lake* at the Théatre des Champs Elysées, 1963, Photograph by A.F.P. from Pictorial Parade Inc. Below, with Yves St. Laurent. Photograph by André Ostier.

An interesting aspect of his life, especially considering the physical demands of dancing, is that he seems to require very little sleep. A few hours at night, and a siesta of a couple of hours in the afternoon, and that is all he needs. Some of his closest friends are insomniacs while he himself is a devotee of TV's late-late movie.

With his fantastic talent, Nureyev has become a significant force in Western ballet, not merely because he makes audiences gasp at the sheer wonder of him all, but because he has had a serious influence upon our dance. Dance historians will have no difficulty in pinpointing the date when Nureyev became transformed from ballet's boy-genius to ballet's man of destiny. It was November 27, 1963, the day of the first performance at the Royal Opera House, Covent Garden, of the Kingdom of the Shades scene from *La Bayadère.* The traditional choreography was by Marius Petipa. But this revival had been directed by Nureyev. He had mounted a few things here and there before, but this was his first major production. He not only provided the Royal Ballet with the right choreography (this an adroit and lucky hack could have done), but also with the right style. He made those English kids dance like Russians.

Clearly the kinship between the Royal Ballet and the Kirov Ballet was close—Nureyev himself felt it; and as the Kirov became known in the West, audiences recognized it. For one thing, there was a considerable similarity in the repertory and, interestingly, the Royal Ballet was still dancing the nineteenth century Maryinsky originals that their one-time owners, the Kirov, had abandoned. *La Bayadère* was regarded in Russia and abroad as the touchstone of the Kirov repertory. How could any company have the effrontery to attempt it, or, for that matter, Nureyev have the nerve to mount it? The Royal Ballet had almost taken its life in its hands and entrusted it to Nureyev. Nureyev's triumph with *La Bayadère* opened up a new career for him—that of producer and coach. In his comparatively short time at the Kirov it is evident that he absorbed everything put in front of him.

He also possesses what is rare but far from unknown in dancers, the ability to remember, kinetically as it were, choreography, and the ability to reproduce not merely one's own role but a complete ballet. Mind you, in all of his Russian reproductions and adaptations, Nureyev has never scorned the use of smuggled Soviet films as an aide-memoire. Yet for the most part his productions really are feats of memory and an uncanny ability to inculcate style and content in dancers, from the ballerinas and their partners, through the coryphees, right down to the corps de ballet. Nureyev has a flair for transmitting these classics, a flair he shares with very few others.

Typically, the first night of *La Bayadère* was not merely a huge success for Nureyev as an artist, it also provided fodder for his bulging gossip column files. Dancing his first variation, he slipped and lost his footing. Where almost every other dancer would have recovered and continued dancing, Nureyev simply stopped and ran off the stage. This was seen as another example of temperament. Was it? Perhaps—undoubtedly in living memory the only dancer to do that on a London stage had been the wayward genius, the French dancer, Jean Babilée, to whom increasingly Nureyev found himself compared. But this stop and start moment could be seen as an aspect of his professionalism, his determination to give his best. Whatever it was, it served to feed the fast-growing Nureyev legend. But then, so did everything else.

As opportunities for Nureyev to dance with other companies—sometimes with Fonteyn, sometimes with another partner—opened up across the world, so also did his new career as a ballet producer burgeon. When he wanted to dance the lead in the full-evening *Don Quixote*, it was necessary for him first to mount the ballet in Vienna and in Australia. Soon he was making a practice of mounting classic ballets.

Each of these productions was based on memories, notes, and films of his Kirov youth, but they also included quite a lot of original choreography. Another famous graduate from the Maryinsky school, George Balanchine, also adapted a great deal from his school days and put on stage such works as *Raymonda Variations*, for example. However much Balanchine adapted and adopted, he called it simply "Balanchine" on the program. Nureyev elected to call his adaptations, perhaps more more modestly, "Petipa, staged by Nureyev," or more rarely, "Nureyev, after Petipa." Still in all these productions there was a certain amount of original choreography. Would Nureyev follow the pattern of his great Leningrad predecessor, Balanchine, and become a choreographer? Nureyev would appear to have a lot in common with Balanchine. Before he came to the West, it was Balanchine who fascinated him the most, and it was Balanchine who served as the motive for dozens and dozens of questions Nureyev would fire off at Western visitors. It was Balanchine about whom he evinced a passionate interest immediately before his defection in Paris.

> . . . *curious and intoxicating feeling when first time I saw* Apollo . . . *Why does he do those strange moves?* . . . *I felt it with Alicia Alonso company* . . . *and it came back to me, when Grigorovich was doing* Legend of Love *on me, and in a general way I said, well, he did this move and that move, and that one, and in a strange way of dancing, this shape and this sound started to open up* . . . *And suddenly, they would open up this symbolism in dance* . . . *in other words become more aloof* . . . *trying to translate* . . . *trying to incorporate images from Persian miniatures into* Legend of Love . . . *so it was kind of wonderful time* . . .

Although Nureyev continued to hold Balanchine in high regard, there was never any question of Nureyev's joining Balanchine's company or even appearing with it as a guest star. Over the years, especially with the Royal Ballet and the Paris Opéra Ballet, Nureyev did manage to dance quite a number of Balanchine roles, notably in *Apollo, The Prodigal Son,* and *Agon.* In 1979 Balanchine created *Le Bourgeois Gentilhomme* for Nureyev, and he danced it with the New York City Opera, and later in Europe.

Nureyev did not follow Balanchine's example and become only a choreographer. For one thing, Nureyev was a far more distinguished dancer than Balanchine had ever been, and his career as a dancer gave little room for choreography. Balanchine concentrated on choreography—luckily for the world—because an injury he suffered as a young man virtually brought his dancing career to a halt. As a choreographer, Nureyev could afford to bide his time. Indeed, he could scarcely afford not to.

Yet, even early on in his days in the West he did make a solitary attempt at original choreography. Typically, it was most unusual. *Tancredi,* to a score by Hans Werner Henze and a story by Peter Csobadi, was first given by the Vienna State Opera Ballet on May 18, 1966. I saw the ballet only once, but its ambitious symbolism impressed me, and it seems as though Nureyev had some original ideas for choreography. However, it was more than ten years before he made another attempt at totally original choreography. This was in 1977 when he staged his own version of Prokofiev's *Romeo and Juliet* for the London Festival Ballet, and even more ambitious undertaking than *Tancredi.* And in 1979 he created *Manfred* for the Paris Opéra Ballet. These works are discussed in a later section of this book.

It has already been stressed that Nureyev's defection was not a political matter. Dancers rarely have the time to feel particularly strongly about politics, and Nureyev's defection was motivated by a strong desire for personal and artistic freedom. Perhaps to an extent this desire for personal liberty can be seen as a political gesture—the Russians would see it as such—but Nureyev was very concerned with the opportunities he needed to develop as an artist.

Just as Nureyev left Ufa to go to Leningrad, so he left Leningrad to go to the rest of the world. I am convinced that Nureyev (and this is also true of many other Russian defectors) would not have left Russia had he been given normal opportunities to work abroad on occasion without difficulties.

He has said "...artistically I found more personal freedom in the West. I have found the freedom to fail, to be pessimistic. All Soviet art has to be optimistic. The sun must always shine. At the end of *Swan Lake,* for example, all must end happily and literally. When I produced *Swan Lake* in Vienna, I had the Prince die at the end. He lost. This was tragic—and tragic in a way that official Soviet art could not understand."

Nureyev is a Romantic dancer in the classic mold, a natural Siegfried or Albrecht; yet his inclination toward modern ballet—demonstrated as much as anything by his own first work *Tancredi*—tended to be avant garde. From the beginning of his time in the West, he was interested in American modern-dance, seeing it as a quite different form of dance expression from the classic ballet he had grown up with, yet at the same time a vigorously expressive kind of dance that possessed its own plastique that was itself a challenge to the young dancer. It was also a time when American modern-dance choreographers were beginning to move into the repertoires of classic ballet companies. Paul Taylor, for example, mounted his work *Aureole* on the Royal Danish Ballet in 1968, an event that even a few years earlier would have been regarded as an impossibility. It was in this atmosphere that Nureyev started to show more than just an interest in American modern-dance but a desire to appear in such ballets.

Taylor's *Aureole* was the first American modern work Nureyev appeared in, and he danced this with the Taylor company, in Mexico and in London. He was also seen during the latter season in Taylor's *Book of Beasts*. He danced in Glen Tetley's *Field Figures* and *Pierrot Lunaire*, and Tetley created roles for him in *Laborintus* and *Tristan*. Othello in José Limón's *The Moor's Pavane* was added to his repertory, and eventually, almost inevitably, he gravitated to the major source of modern-dance today, Martha Graham. He took classes with her and appeared with her company in repertory roles in *Night Journey*, *El Penitente*, *Clytemnestra*, *Ecuatorial*, and as the Revivalist Preacher in *Appalachian Spring*. Two works, *Lucifer* (in the premiere of which Fonteyn also appeared) and *The Scarlet Letter*, were actually created for Nureyev by Graham. Later, Murray Louis was to create three works for him: *Moment*, *Vivace*, and *The Canarsie Venus*.

As Nureyev matured, grew older, he wanted to dance more and more and more. His ideal would be to dance six or even seven times a week, sometimes full-evening roles. With this in mind, his manager, S.A. Gorlinsky, arranged tours with such companies as the Australian Ballet, the National Ballet of Canada, and the London Festival Ballet, where Nureyev would dance the leading role virtually every night during a long tour, often with a revolving roster of company ballerinas. In effect, the companies in question were becoming supporting ensembles for the star. It was a procedure that caused a lot of comment, much of it unfavorable.

Another way of catering to Nureyev's need to be seen and his public's desire to see him was a series of programs arranged by Gorlinsky called *Nureyev and Friends*. These programs were extremely varied and passed through a number of versions. Nureyev appeared—and he has presented these programs in New York, Washington, D.C., London,

Paris, and various other European cities—with a group of dancers in a sort of smorgasbord of programs designed to show off Nureyev, who usually danced every single ballet during the programs, in a variety of roles and guises.

There are very few dancers who sell tickets in a mass market, and these few vary slightly across the world. For example, Maya Plisetskaya could sell out in Paris or New York, but is not a particularly big star in London; Nureyev is still at the peak of his popularity in New York and internationally, and, although without a permanent base in London, he has packed London's largest theater, the Coliseum, for weeks on end each summer since his long season there of 1976.

This popularity has partly to do with his dancing—there are people who believe that he is the greatest dancer of the twentieth century, and virtually everyone is agreed that he belongs to the top handful—yet it has also to do with the way he has impinged upon public consciousness. He never courts publicity, but then he never has to. It seems to come to him quite naturally, like iron filings to a magnet.

After all these years of dancing, the fervor with which he approaches dance is absolutely unabated. Indeed, as he advances in his career, he tends to dance more rather than less, and the sheer number of performances he gives over the years savors something of compulsion. Many people have questioned what makes Rudolf run. It is not money, although like most people who were once very poor, he has a kind of regard for its value and for the status it can endow. But this hardly explains his fixation, his determination to go on dancing even when sick or injured, the backbreaking schedules he permits for himself, the incredible amount of work he gets through in a month, in a year. Probably no dancer has ever worked so hard and so consistently as Nureyev. At times it seems as though even a brief vacation is an unwelcome diversion from his main objective in life—dancing.

Probably the main cause of Nureyev's obsession is simply his realization of the tragic brevity, comparatively speaking, of a dancer's performing career and his determination to stretch that career as far as it can be stretched. He is also physically the kind of dancer who thrives on work. He feels that he actually improves with overwork, and, although the fashionable thing to say is that he is "burning himself out" with excessive appearances, there is some justification for his view that this onerous performance load helps his performances rather than hinders them.

Well, there is very simple economic thing. . .there is a certain commercialism you have to sacrifice yourself to. . .financially it is more feasible for a company. The company has to pay for itself, to pay for the pleasure of my coming to New York or to London, or going to Australia, or somewhere else. I have to pay with my presence, by being on stage, I have to pay for the pleasure of doing those cities. . .you cannot say I can do only three performances or five performances. . .there is kind of technical thing too, I do dance better if I dance five times a week. . .but look at the Balanchine company, they dance everyday, they dance eight times a week, maybe not so much. . .but then they also don't have the emotional feeling that they are responsible, and it is difficult. . .but it is easier from the responsibility point of view, the whole thing depending on you. . .so you do it. . .you do your best. . .you have to be involved.

At first, I was wondering often, how those Broadway people could perform every day for six months or two years, and maybe more—this puzzled me. . .and then the first time. . . it was the fourth or fifth time the Royal Ballet came back to New York. . .people would start falling ill . . .and first I danced four times a week, then it was packed, absolutely. . .and I did six times a week. . .and suddenly I saw it is possible. . .then I found out I am dancing better than when I am dancing less. . .so by then I get used to the lights, I get used to the this and that. . . I am not just cross-eyed and petrified with what I am doing. . . I knew what I was going to do, and just did it!

His mind has always been totally open and he apparently absorbs like a sponge. He had not been in the West for more than a month before he was dressing at the peak of mod fashion—a small point, but it illuminatingly shows his chameleon powers of adaptation. This quality of adaptation has been critical to his artistic growth. His willingness to dance in modern works shows that he has gone a long way since he solemnly informed me in 1962 that "I am a Romantic dancer." Yes, Romantic; and many things more.

A wary, cautious, and generous man, he has yet to pass into the next phase of his career, which will be attaching himself, in one way or another, to an institution. So far he has been a freelance dancer and producer, and he has never really put down roots. He is said to have a tidy bank account, and he has on occasion occupied a number of homes, houses, and apartments. But the nearest thing he has made to a career commitment has been his years with the Royal Ballet. Eventually his career will lead him to running his own company; at least one would expect this to be the pattern. As a dancer in his forties, he can expect five or ten years' activity—perhaps a little more, perhaps a little less. The time will come when he will have to decide what direction he is going to give to his career. This is not really to be discussed here, for it is the concern of a later section of the book. The likelihood is that he will direct some dance company and that his effect on international dance might well only have just started.

THE ARTIST

I think that, at root, every dancer in the world—certainly every male dancer—can quite swiftly trace his genealogical tree back to Auguste Vestris. It may seem incredible, but any dancer can. Although there have been fundamentally three different styles of teaching—the French, later transformed into the Franco-Danish, the Italian, and the Russian—all three have become deeply intermingled over the generations. I would say that one of the salient things that has happened in contemporary ballet is the international ascendancy of the Soviet style as codified by Agrippina Vaganova. It was based on the old Russian style, which in turn drew on the Franco-Danish style with contributions, for example, from the Swedish dancer and teacher Christian Johanssen, one of Bournonville's pupils, who was to be critically important to Russian ballet. Of course, the impact of Enrico Cecchetti and the Italian style had a considerable effect on Russian ballet, too. But during the twenties, it was really Vaganova who wove together the separate strands—tending, for example, to eradicate and even erase the sharper differences between the Moscow and the St. Petersburg styles so that dancers of the Bolshoi and the Kirov today—although there is still a difference between them—show it less than in the past.

You know, at the Kirov, everything is best, writers, creators—Kirov's writers were always more creative than Bolshoi's . . . Bolshoi practically never created anything. There it was the question of maintaining their classical repertory . . . At Kirov there was always the spring board, there was always that past, which was there, from which they could propel, which they did not have to invent, because it was there . . . As a result they had Goleizovsky they had Lopoukhov, and we have Balanchine . . . Jacobson, a little bit . . . all the way back . . . then you have Grigorovich . . . and they all come from this rich traditional classical repertory of Petipa . . . and Bolshoi did not have it, they really did not have any formal productions . . . everything was simply borrowed . . .

By now, virtually all classic dancing has gathered itself into a single, flowing stream. Occasionally you will catch a glimpse, even a vision of a reversion to a specific style. For

In *Swan Lake*. Photograph by Anthony Crickmay.

example, in the Franco-Danish style as seen in Bournonville, the Danish heritage, the *ports de bras* is absolutely straight, almost alien to the more sophisticated sense of epaulement that the Russians have developed to such a considerable degree.

Nureyev started dancing late. Of course he had a background of folk dance, but he came to classical dancing late. The influence of Pushkin on him was decisive. I think that Nureyev is not your simple, pure stylist and technician. It is almost as if he acts a style rather than possesses it, and this was particularly true when he was younger. He had a terrific grace, an animal magnetism which revealed itself in the pantherine-like jump, which was one of his hallmarks during what one might call his first phase of performing.

If you have seen photographs of Nureyev in performance, most of his positions look perfect. Nureyev is careful about photographs; he even tears them up if he does not like them. When he can, he makes sure that photographs showing ungraceful positions are not used. This was a tactic he learned from Fonteyn. Yet I would say that in even his first period, there was a certain lack of cohesion in transitional moments that you would not note with such consummate stylists and technicians as Bruhn, Baryshnikov, Bujones, or Dowell. Nureyev's artistic strengths lie slightly elsewhere. Yes, he really is a Romantic dancer—he is a dancer of image, of impact, of emotional suggestion and expressive power. The interest of Nureyev as a dancer lies not so much in his style or his technique as in his phenomenal ability to project an image, a capacity I suspect very few dancers have ever possessed—although certainly Nijinsky obviously had it.

The study of acting was part of the curriculum at the Vaganova School. Years ago when I first interviewed Nureyev on his first time on British television, I asked him about Stanislavsky and the Stanislavsky influence. He said: "I regard Stanislavsky as one of the earliest of my teachers. I am a Romantic dancer." Dance students in Russia are given acting lessons in a way that Western dancers are not. The American system, in particular, is based much more on the procedures of the ballet class. In Russia, dancers are instructed thoroughly in mime, in pure acting, and in other theatrical areas as well. They take classes in music and art history. The aesthetic education they receive is substantial and rounded.

Nureyev was not just *any* dancer; he was ever, and supremely, an individualist. His character bore always the stamp of the rebel, the absolute seal of one not content with what he was being given. Early on, he had been extremely fortunate to come under the care and attention of Alexander Pushkin, one of the greatest teachers and coaches ballet has even known, responsible for the training of Nureyev and Baryshnikov as well as a whole generation of other, remarkably fine male dancers.

In *Laurencia.* Royal Ballet 1965. Photograph by Reg Wilson.

I never saw Nureyev in Pushkin's class; I did see Baryshnikov with him. Yet it is singular to note how totally different they are as dancers, although Pushkin probably had the single, most vital formative impact on each one's career, on each one's style and manner. People are always venturing into comparisons between Nureyev and Baryshnikov when, in fact, such an enterprise is perhaps the most irrelevant futility in contemporary ballet. Each is unique, utterly and absolutely, yet each was formed and nurtured, not only by the same system, but by the same teacher.

In this connection it must be pertinent, however obvious, to say that one became a Dionysus and the other an Apollo. The greatest male dancers do tend to embody these particular incarnations of dance—the Apollonian and the Dionysiac. Oddly enough, most of the great male dancers gravitate towards the Apollonian. In our own time, Erik Bruhn, Anthony Dowell, Peter Martins, Helgi Tomasson—all are Apollonian embodiments. In assessing a distinction here, not any mere superiority, the Dionysiac dancer seems to be distinctly rarer. Nijinsky must have been a quintessential Dionysiac. Edward Villella was; certainly Rudolf Nureyev is.

With Anya Linden in *Flower Festival at Genzano* pas de deux, Royal Ballet. Photograph from the Theatre Museum, Houston Rogers Collection (Victoria and Albert Museum, London).

With Nadia Nerina in *Laurencia*. Photograph by Anthony Crickmay.

The Apollonian reality is interpreted by some as embodying more of the ideal, even the ethereal, while the Dionysiac is taken as implying more potent roots in the earth. It seems to me rather that the extraordinary inner fire emanating from such rare vessels of the Dionysiac as Nijinsky and Villella and Nureyev—their inextricable blend of the carnal and the spiritual—stands in sharp contrast to the texture and consistency of cool aloofness that is the hallmark of the Apollonian. It is not simply a question of the mime; what matters is the outline, the entire essence and impact—the image is crucial—of the performance. Nor do I think it is a question of some larger or deeper or more profound search in one direction or another. Indeed, I think it may be quite simply that when we speak of Apollonian and Dionysiac, we might also easily say Classical and Romantic.

Ultimately, it is a question of involvement with the audience, a question of the presentation of the dancer's self. We take some artists to be deeply subjective; others appear to us supremely objective. For example, in the Balanchine ballets *Apollo* and *The Prodigal Son*, you might expect Nureyev to be an ideal Prodigal Son and barely an adequate Apollo. In sober fact, he is a superb Apollo and a very good Prodigal Son.

Perhaps it cuts even more deeply, and the issue becomes one of the dancer's evaluation of himself, his attempt to understand precisely what and who he is. I think Baryshnikov regards himself primarily as a curator of the dance. Nureyev, I think, regards himself as an image of The Dance itself.

For Nureyev *does* go beyond. He is ever the romantic, the subjective, the solitary person trying to stretch his art in a uniquely personal way. He is not interested in providing a textbook primer of classic dance; he is attempting, rather, to project a very private and individual image of the self. For example, when some dancers perform Albrecht, they try to dance Albrecht as they think Albrecht might have danced Albrecht. Nureyev always tries to dance Albrecht as he thinks Nureyev would dance Albrecht. He never really wants to lose himself, even though often—and supremely—he does; what interests him is the projection of himself, at the highest pitch, within the terms of acting.

Here one might cite the obvious distinction between Olivier and Gielgud. Everything that Laurence Olivier has ever done has had on it the stamp of Olivier. This is not a criticism; it is, I think, marvelous. Everything that John Gielgud has done has borne less the stamp of Gielgud than the stamp of his taste, his finesse, his personality and skill. Gielgud is much more of an instrument. Olivier is much more of a force.

Nureyev, too, with his pioneering in dance, his proselytizing and extravagant spending of himself, is equally a force. Yet his talents often strike me as enigmatically contradictory, sometimes turning in upon him curiously. In some fashion, this great flamboyant personality is always in dialogue with itself. Perhaps the specialness of the Russian temperament may account for that. I know that Nureyev is a Tatar and a Moslem, but his behavior is, at times, quite remarkably Russian. He *looks* like a Tatar; he does not look very Russian. Baryshnikov, Soloviev, Vasiliev—to the eye, all visibly more Russian. No Nureyev does not look Russian. There is that Oriental cast to him—the look, oddly enough, that Nijinsky had, the look that can be seen so clearly in Bakst's famous gouache of him in the *Danse Siamoise*.

Some people resent what they take as Nureyev's personal arrogance, objecting to what they see as a lack of modesty. I would not describe him as "modest," but I do think he possesses humility. Neither would I describe him as "arrogant." He is a perfectionist, and so strong is that streak in him, that at times he seems to equate the imperfect with the immoral. His character is a difficult one to understand, hence much misunderstood. I think he is a man peculiarly driven by circumstances, hurled by ambition and the simple desire to excel. Yet he is certainly a man extraordinarily generous, extraordinarily loyal, willing to share his artistic experience with other dancers. He has proven that time and time again.

He is certainly not arrogant as an artist. It is well known that he has been difficult with partners, but sometimes partners have been difficult with him. And he is willing to forgive. He is also an oddly nervous person. Probably all dancers, when they take that first step on stage, feel their hearts turn to chaos. This is certainly true of Nureyev. He is a reserved, even shy person with a profound impulse and the impulsive desire to create something, to bring something into conceptual being. On one level it may be to create an image—on the larger scale, it may be to move that image into realization of the ballet. He is clearly concerned with the creative process, and when people stand in the way of that goal, he has been known to get unusually angry.

Nureyev is also somewhat uncertain of himself. The charming yet vicious uncertainty of artists, the difficulty they have in achieving what they think and know they are capable of, is an element in them that we occasionally underestimate. For example, I've noticed that some artists read literally everything written about them; others ignore all notices, commentary, and criticism. Nureyev reads it all; he even pays serious attention to the words of persons he may actually despise.

It is a curious enigma: he is one of the most vulnerable of people, and that very vulnerability is one of the qualities that makes it difficult for him to work with other artists. He has his great and special loyalties; moreover, he extends his personal code of loyalty into his professional life—something as unusual in dancers as it is in all performing artists. He has his favorite ballerinas, and time and again, he has shown a creative involvement with their careers.

The dancing relationship he had with Fonteyn was certainly the zenith of both of their performing lives. There was a special magic to Fonteyn and Nureyev in performance that seemed to spark the imagination of the world in rather the same fashion that Nijinsky and Karsavina together had ignited the imagination of an earlier generation. Something about that relationship for Nureyev was distinctly different. But he has had relationships with other ballerinas that have proved artistically remarkable and mutually enriching. Often he has come under fire as some kind of supreme egotist in his dancing partnerships, but I have never met a ballerina who was not enormously grateful for the way in which he gave *her*, and her alone, the full credit. He enhances a ballerina, glorifies and worships her in a way that few male dancers do. And his generosity extends to male dancers as well, with an influence that goes far beyond his example and his teaching or the enormity of his impact on the world's awareness of the male in dance.

Nureyev's projection of himself as a dancer is what I find most remarkable about him as an artist: his ability simultaneously to lose himself *in* a role and yet impose himself *on* that role. As I have observed, that is a gift he shares almost uniquely (I know that nothing grammatically can be "almost unique," but simply look at the evidence) with Laurence Olivier. Although everything he does is unmistakably Nureyev—with the accent, the tone, the signature of Nureyev—he gives always to each of those roles its particular stamp. In this he is not only the Dionysiac presence we have already contemplated; he is equally Prometheus, the fire-bringer.

I am constantly amazed, for example, at the difference he brings to his Albrecht in *Giselle* and his Prince Siegfried in *Swan Lake*. Every major male dancer has in his basic repertoire a classic "Prince" conception. It is usually noble, with a certain *hauteur* and glamour; it moves around the stage with elegance and a kind of debonair hopefulness. It indeed announces by every gesture: "I am the Prince."

Nureyev is different. He seeks out a psychological resonance in such roles. Take his Albrecht. Albrecht is spoiled, vain, something of a fop; he is a young, totally irresponsible man who is suddenly shaken into a Pushkin-style tragedy and that realization of himself by the death of a peasant girl with whom he has been almost casually in love. Nureyev gives Albrecht just that Pushkin-like horror and stab—precisely that Pushkin of *Eugene Onegin*, all of whose heroes are given to such violent, abrupt change—and he endows his portrayal with startling honesty. A matador's moment of truth.

Most dancers play Siegfried in much the same way as they play Albrecht, only this time the man is finding love with a myth rather than a woman. Nureyev cuts into the role most decisively. At first, he gives us an almost playful Siegfried, certainly a more sympathetic prince than his companion portrait of Albrecht. This Siegfried is a spirited young man who does not want to get married, but who falls in love with Odette, becomes remote and withdrawn, ill at ease among his court. At the end of *Swan Lake*, he has been transformed less by

With Sonia Arova in *Swan Lake*, Royal Ballet. Photograph by Anthony Crickmay.

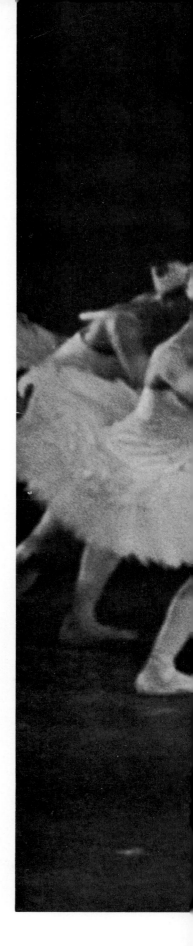

With Margot Fonteyn in *Swan Lake.* Left, photograph by Georgina Villacorte; above, photograph by Judy Cameron.

tragedy than by love. Nureyev has presented us with rather a different prince, and a different destiny from the destiny and the prince he created for us in *Giselle.*

One marvels at Nureyev's ability to infuse humanity into such figures.

. . .with age, of course, cynicism creeps in and in a way you probably arrive to the original reading. . .from that true love which will depart, from that very true love. . .through the useful years, to something more cynical. . .

You sense all the time that Nureyev is thinking not just about the steps or the dancing, but about the role. For example, he insisted on inserting into act one of *Swan Lake* a solo for Siegfried—rather like one of Hamlet's soliloquies—in which you see the quintessential romantic prince alone, distressed, melancholy.

The Prince is a romantic man: that is why I retained that solo at the beginning in the first act, in which he seems more pathetic. . . It was there initially, but was rediscovered, it was really there, written by Tchaikovsky, and Petipa of course sanctioned it. . .

You can see his same imagination at work in the surprisingly complex character Nureyev makes out of Jean de Brienne in *Raymonda.* Above all, you can see it in *The Sleeping Beauty* where *he* comes on, and suddenly the complete and perfect poet out of Petrarch is before you. Nureyev makes the audience marvel at his dancing, but even more, he draws it into seeing his partner through the character's (his own) eyes. This is a power that very few other dancers have ever possessed.

Nureyev's absorption—even self-absorption—in his art, in dance, is wholly remarkable. I once reminded him of a story I had heard ". . .about you rehearsing *Giselle* by yourself on the stage at Covent Garden, and the opera company had to move in, and you had to move out. . .you moved out without a question. . .but there was a look of sadness on your face as if you seemed to be finding something in the part you might never find again. . ."

His private life is spasmodic, more like a shadow to his stage life than his stage life is the shadow of his real life. He lives almost more intensely on the stage than he does off it. In the daily world, he does not try to impress; conceivably the only person he is trying to impress— to convince—is himself. For someone who lives so much of his life on a stage, he is a supremely natural presence, utterly spontaneous in his reactions. In recent years, he has learned patience and that Western veneer of politeness he lacked at one time; he has learned, too, the vagaries of the English language, and its subtleties, which he uses exceptionally well. Yet, even so, he is prepared always to say what he wants and to do what he wants.

With Svetlana Beriosova in the Black Swan pas de deux on NBC *London Palladium Show,* 1966. Photograph by United Press International.

He is a peculiarly difficult person to get to know—it may take years—yet he is a warm friend, one who guards that friendship most carefully. He is not expansive; he is reluctant to let people know he is their friend—he would prefer them to believe and to trust. There have been a number of strong and durable personal relationships in his life. However, most have been fugitive. One feels that personal affinities have rarely meant as much to him as they do to most people. Yet this could be the inevitable consequence of the questing thrust of his nature.

Nureyev is insatiably curious. It has always been a source of intriguing speculation to me as to what might have happened to him had he remained in the Soviet Union. What could have happened? Certainly there would have been no obvious opportunity to satisfy that incessant curiosity. Nureyev has a nature very akin to that of George Balanchine, for whom the necessity to leave Russia was an inevitable movement of his spirit—for both the impulse to know, to experience, and to dare was simply too potent to be denied.

Money, was not and is not a primary element for Nureyev. The freedom it provides him is important, and what counts for Nureyev is freedom. Yet even in the West his freedom is so restrained and contained by his ambition that he sometimes seems to me to be one of the least free persons I know.

Perhaps the major force behind what really does "make Rudolf run" is the unquenchable demand of that special, unending desire for experience, and his compulsive obsession with dance experience. Nureyev is possessed with an imperative need to use his body in almost every conceivable style of dance. That is why he probably could never have survived in the Soviet Union. The intensity and range of his imagination would never have submitted to those restrictions. In my view, it is probable that he may be the most imaginative dancer the world has ever been privileged to know.

Whenever one thinks of Rudolf Nureyev's unique position in the dance world, one has to think of his sheer dance prowess. Simply, how good a dancer is he? Or, how good a dancer was he?

Nureyev's powers of projection, of sheer showmanship, have always been evident, and in some respects these may have detracted from the just evaluation of his technique, particularly as a young dancer. However, when he first performed such ballets as *La Bayadère* or in the pas de deux from *Le Corsaire*, the effectiveness of his technique was almost overwhelming. The speed and elevation he exhibited in his early days had probably never been surpassed, and his performances instantly revived the legend of Nijinsky. It was soon evident that Nureyev was going to cause more interest in dance than any of his contemporaries. At first that interest concentrated upon the front-page drama of his defection, but it spread over

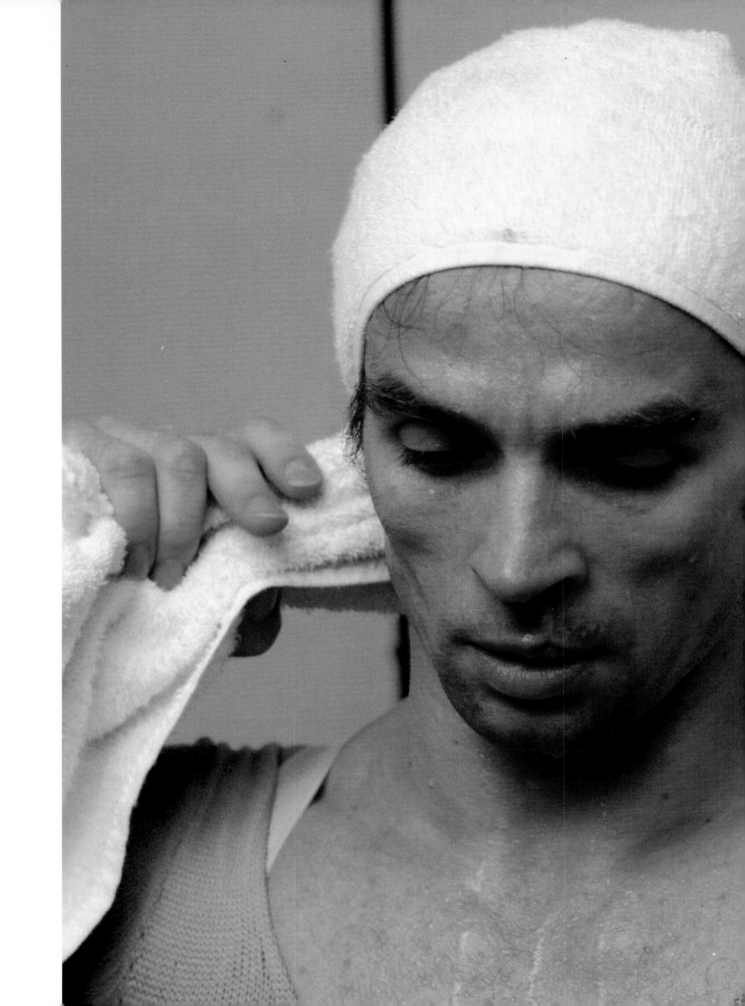

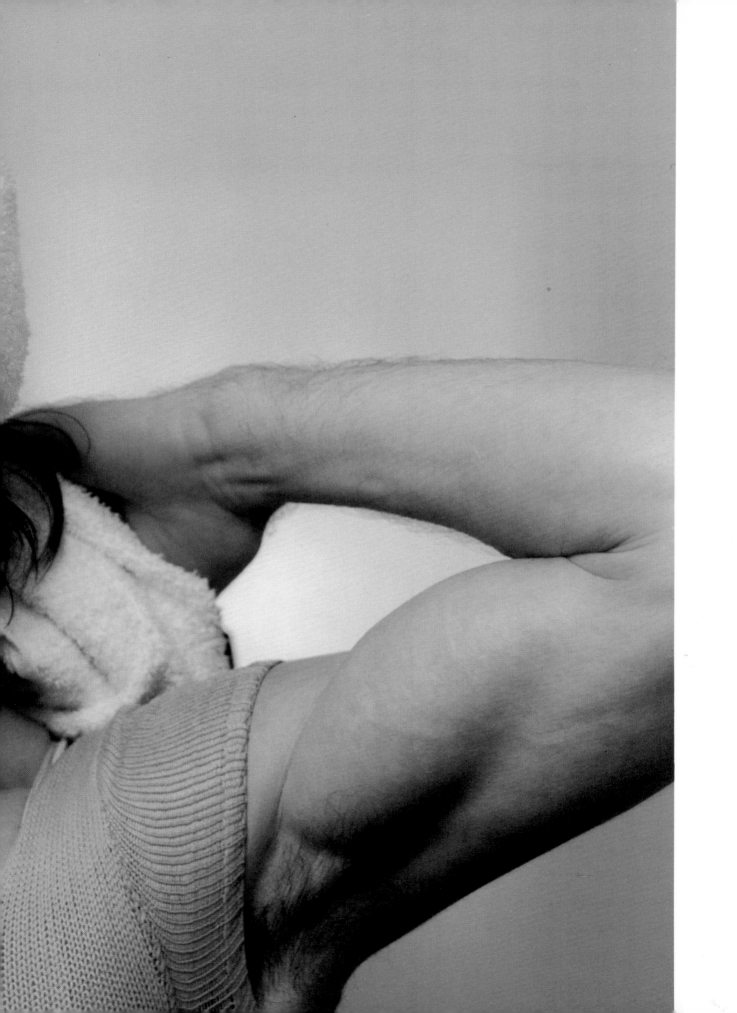

into the nature of his dancing—he was soon talked of as the most sensational dancer alive, and audiences were led to regard him at first as some kind of phenomenon, or even freak, of show business. No one would suggest that this was a healthy attitude. The surprising thing is that Nureyev did not disappoint even those sensation seekers. There was almost a quantitative measure of athletic prowess about his dancing in those early days that fulfilled almost every extravagant expectation of wonderment.

This partially uncritical adulation did not affect his performances or his entire approach to his art. Through all of this presumably unsettling period he remained virtually untouched and, at least as a dancer, unchanged. He made no concessions to cheapen his dancing, no lowering of his standards, no attempts to cash in on the public taste for pure physical sensationalism. Most critics in the West recognized the superior nature of Nureyev's artistry. No, the quality of his dancing was never in question.

Nureyev has always suffered from over-exposure. Even in Russia he was a sort of wunderkind—Alexander Pushkin's favorite pupil—the wild Tatar child who could not quite accommodate himself to the "normality" of the Kirov.

In recent years it has not been news to suggest that Nureyev is not dancing very well. The only news is that Nureyev is not dancing *his best,* that he is stretching himself too thin, doing too much, and quite naturally, like all of us, getting older. In 1982 he is forty-four. He is one of those lonely Russian long-distance runners; and his age—here and now—is both superbly relevant and superbly irrelevant. Yes, there will come a time when age will catch up with him. Although the chances are that he will continue on stage in some capacity, the days of crazy fervor and virtuosity will have run out like unremitting sand. What will remain will be a series of images caught in the mind's eye, a few films, a museum collection of photographs, and a garland of criticisms, attempts to recall and make real what is forever beyond remembering.

The special quality of Nureyev's dancing has always been emblematic. You see Nureyev on stage, and the character he creates, even the figure he cuts, lingers in the memory. I remember well my first sight of him in 1961 at the Drury Lane Theatre in London. At the very first London appearance, almost all the elements that were to make up Nureyev's eventual stage persona were in evidence. His technical prowess was shown off admirably in the *Black Swan* pas de deux with Rosella Hightower. Admittedly on that occasion, the young man was a trifle nervous and perhaps did not do himself complete justice—but it was justice enough. Manifestly, he was an artist of the most unusual quality; and the stories from Russia and from Paris, where he had defected only several weeks earlier, had not been exaggerated. The man was a phenomenon. It was the Ashton solo, *Poème Tragique* to music by Scriabin, that really demonstrated the Nureyev essence, and what he was going to bring to the West. It was to be total involvement, total commitment to a role, an approach to the business of ballet-making akin to Stanislavsky in its intensity. He hurtled onto the Drury Lane stage like a frenzied animal. What Ashton had created for him was fairly simple, but the choreographer had recognized instantly the dancer's special qualities of moving, of standing still, and most of all, of projecting a character. In virtually one rehearsal Ashton had discovered Nureyev's secret. It was not simply that he jumped higher or moved faster than any of his contemporaries—although indeed he probably did. What Nureyev possessed uniquely was the ability to impose an image on the stage. That is why his performances live so long in the memory and why, once he has appeared in a role, even if the appearance is almost casual, he seems to leave an indelible imprint on both memory and the role.

For example, he danced the leading male role in *Symphonic Variations* only once with the Royal Ballet. Yet he left his mark on the role. I remember him in it in a way I cannot remember certain other dancers who performed it on many more occasions. Nureyev has a gift for being memorable.

In many respects this is simply because he eliminates almost all extraneous matter from his performance. I recall the first time I saw him dance Albrecht in *Giselle* with Margot Fonteyn. It has been said that when he was in Russia, Nureyev always dreamt of dancing in England at Covent Garden with Margot Fonteyn, and in *Giselle*. Well, that dream came true. Nureyev's conquest at Covent Garden in *Giselle* on February 21, 1962 might have been predictable but could hardly have been more complete. His dancing combined elegance and breadth in a way I had never seen before. His elevation and ballon were remarkable not only in themselves, but remarkable in the way they were used. Everyone had already noted his splendid elevation, but he proved a stronger, lighter, and far neater dancer than his only previous London appearance in that hurly burly of the Drury Lane Gala might have suggested. His dancing had the catlike spring and bite that I expected, coupled with all the mellifluous flow and beautiful phrasing one could wish for. Unquestionably he proved himself a dancer of immense potentiality. Dancing Albrecht opposite Fonteyn's Giselle, he got under the skin of the part as the Stanislavsky disciple he is. His stage presence was remarkable, and audiences responded to him in a great tidal wave of communication that seemed to wash over the theater when he entered.

There may be those who will suggest, either now or at some time in the future, that Nureyev triumphed because of his publicity. On the contrary, he triumphed *despite* his publicity. Unquestionably, a great star had arrived in the world of ballet—and one, moreover, capable of exerting a considerable influence upon the art.

Nureyev did not offer any simple interpretation of Albrecht. With a slightly mocking smile—a smile, by the way, that you can detect also in photographs of Nijinsky in the role—

Nureyev wandered through the entire ballet like an explorer possessed by a character. He never seemed to make any attempt to play Albrecht. He did not have to, for he so clearly embodied Albrecht that acting would have seemed irrelevant.

Nureyev's portrayal of Albrecht at this first English performance proved convincing and subtle. The sly, charming villain of the first act, a feckless dallying aristocrat, stood out as a delicately etched portrait. At these first performances it must be admitted that Nureyev's often small-scaled and always naturalistic acting was occasionally at odds with the formal semaphore mime favored by the Royal Ballet. At times it looked disconcertingly as though Nureyev was, as it were, appearing in Chekhov while most of his colleagues were acting out some kind of English melodrama, most of the cast gesturing in rhetorical bombast. Nureyev's simple naturalistic acting seemed nearly over-casual. Here one would ultimately concede that everyone was out of step except Nureyev.

In 1962 Nureyev told me: "In the West they use old mime which was born a long time ago. In Russia they had it also, but they forget it after the big influence of Stanislavsky. Now when you study some character in your performance, you are obliged to find a basis for each movement, and without this it could have no truth. You believe through your whole movement—otherwise it is immediately seen by audience and everybody that it's wrong."

First, there is a question of style... Swan Lake *demands a certain style,* Giselle *something else,* Sleeping Beauty *something else...the background, the status...this was very clearly explained...all their neuroses...like in* Swan Lake, *he was moody and that is why he could have the confusion... Though they denied aristocracy, somehow they did make clear that the Prince was exceptional character: he was exceptional man; it does not happen just to everybody to see there are swans...*

The Russians are right. The only way to make *Giselle* a living ballet for our times is to acknowledge that Albrecht, not Giselle, is the central character. Franco Zeffirelli once sketched out to me his theory that the great heroes of literature are perennially modern men. He cited Don Juan to support his honest fantasy. Albrecht is equally a "modern" man, and his deceptions and agonies are things we can understand. Giselle probably means much less to us. There is nothing particularly revelatory about a jilted girl having her heart broken, and although Giselle offers the opportunity for great and convincing acting, it is acting which clearly must transcend the novelette character rather than illuminate it.

Nureyev approached Albrecht historically, recognizing in him the feudal aristocrat. This must be understood that the social reality governs his actions and permits him to do nothing outside this basic conception. He offers us a thoughtless, irresponsible youth rapturously, madly in love with Giselle. He deceives her, but Albrecht's drama, as Nureyev sees it,

With Karen Kain in *Giselle*, National Ballet of Canada, 1978. Photograph by Louis Péres. Below, the final moment of *Giselle*. La Scala Opera Ballet, 1981. Photograph by William J. Reilly.

Rehearsing *Giselle* with Carla Fracci, 1971. Photograph by Pitre Agency Photo Press.

is one of regeneration through tragic love. Albrecht, an aristocratic philanderer, caught up in enraptured youthful love for the village belle Giselle, is still securely bound to his lawful fiancée from the court, but is shocked into the realization of a deeper love by Giselle's madness and death.

Almost with one expression of heartfelt agony, Nureyev contrived to suggest Albrecht's first realization of responsibility and pain. The manner in which, in the course of one brief scene, he moved spiritually from mere petulance to heroic grief was to be ballet acting at its finest.

Comparing Nureyev's Albrecht to Erik Bruhn's was persistently fascinating and interesting. Bruhn did not trouble to be different from his dancing rivals; he contented himself with being better. Here he was the conventional lover, betrayer, penitent, all conveyed with intense force. After Giselle's death, Bruhn's Albrecht erupted into mad hysteria, not the polite coloratura histrionics of the romantic lyric theater, but the real thing, stark and raving. It was as shocking as though someone suddenly began to play Strindberg in the middle of Oscar Wilde. During these years, Bruhn was a constant inspiration, stimulus, and rival to Nureyev. He pushed him forward, and he taught him a new type of dramatic expression, together with a new conception of classic elegance.

When Nureyev's Albrecht is saved from the spectral furies by the all-forgiving love of the wraith Giselle in act two, he comes to terms with himself and with reality. The romanticism of the second act found Nureyev in his element, his hair disheveled, his cheeks hollowed, and his eyes burning with a hopeless passion. Yet he appeared entirely credible, not least in the elegiac grace of his first entrance when searching for Giselle's grave. Nothing justified Nureyev's claim—"I am a Romantic dancer"—more powerfully than that entrance. Consumed with grief and guilt, transfigured by tragedy, he played the whole second act like a man in a trance, watching visions, a man divorced from the material world. The full force of the conception only made itself felt at the end when the bewildered yet mature Albrecht is left alone in contemplation. A boy has come to tragic maturity.

Sixteen years later in a review of *Giselle,* I found myself writing of this masterly conception: "Nureyev is the only dancer I know who seems to improve with what would normally be thought of as overwork...his dancing seems to have the same elasticity and bite that it had a decade ago, while the maturity of his interpretations gives them a new classic depth. This is great dancing, but also consummate acting."

I remarked to him in 1977: "...but you always find something new in these parts... you tend to develop them...and to work at them." He replied:

Oh, you cannot stay...and I could not force myself to think the same way that I thought at the age of twenty-one when I did it...with Kolpakova, and with Shelest...

The role of Prince Florimund in *The Sleeping Beauty* is one that has always been closely associated with Nureyev. He achieved great acclaim in the ballet in Leningrad, and it was in this same role that he made his Paris debut with the Kirov Ballet. After he defected, it was again in the Florimund role in addition to the Bluebird that he appeared in the curious de Cuevas production mounted by Raymundo de Larrain.

It was not until May 17, 1962 that Nureyev made his London debut as Florimund. He partnered the French ballerina, Yvette Chauviré. Chauviré, who had danced the role in London four years before, was in fairness then not at her best; also in fairness, she was not particularly helped by her partnership with the young Russian. There seemed to be little rapport between them, and their individual talents stubbornly refused to blend. London was expecting a great deal, particularly after Nureyev's first sensational success in the West with the role. At this London performance it was both easy and difficult to see how that success happened. His stage presence was as electric as ever, yet his brooding characterization

With Merle Park in *The Sleeping Beauty*, Royal Ballet. Photograph by Zoë Dominic.

proved too much in one key. He looked the part of the romantic hero to perfection—or would have had he worn a wig—bareheaded he appeared oddly unfinished among the well-coiffed courtiers. His partnering was at worst casual, and at best, emotionally too withdrawn. His dancing in places looked carelessly brilliant. But when he entered his solo with that circle of marvelously sustained vertiginous jumps, one had a fascinating glimpse of a unique dancer. Obviously Nureyev was never going to be a prince merely of whirls and twirls. He was able to walk on the stage with a poetic deliberation that had an artless artistry.

As an artist, Nureyev might have been born to dance Prince Siegfried in *Swan Lake*. He made his debut in the role with the Royal Ballet at the Royal Opera House on the 22nd of June, 1962. Oddly enough, he was not partnering Margot Fonteyn, but the Bulgarian-born ballerina, Sonia Arova. In many respects this first performance as Siegfried produced the same kind of sensation that his Albrecht had provoked when he danced it with Fonteyn.

At first his portrayal was less rewarding than his Albrecht, partly I suspect because he had made an unresolved compromise between the Soviet and Western approaches to the role. This is oddly symbolized in the third act, when he wore the black tunic of the Western Siegfried together with the white tights every Soviet Siegfried keeps in his wardrobe. His black and white prince looked bizarre, neither one thing nor the other. He had made many changes in the production and the choreography, changes that mortally offended much of the English dance world, who considered their version—the Ivanov/Petipa heritage brought from Russia by Nicolai Sergeyev—a treasure preserved only in Britain.

Nureyev's early performances of Siegfried had a quality of excitement one would perhaps look for in vain elsewhere in ballet. His dancing was far from perfect—although less far than his more partisan detractors would have suggested—but he performed with such an air of rapture that it would have been an unfeeling heart that was not moved. This was an immature, undisciplined Siegfried, and it is not altogether irrelevant that Nureyev needed a haircut; however, with his gothic bloom and romantic yearnings, he was a Siegfried that haughtily struck at the heart of the matter. Like Bruhn before him, he was melancholy in the first act. In the second act he seemed the personification of the romantic hero. One began to see that he identified with—rather than acted—a part. His presence and personality were immense, his dancing a string of marvelous moments.

It was a performance that was rewarded with red roses thrown from the gallery and twenty-one curtain calls. The reception swept aside any lingering doubts that Nureyev was the major event in the postwar ballet world. With his shaggy wind-swept hair, hectic brilliance, and Byronic allure, he instantly created a Prince Siegfried of wild, fanatic quality. Seeing him in his most extended role yet, no one could doubt that he had immense star appeal. There had not been another Rudolf like this since Valentino.

Curtain call with Margot Fonteyn after a Royal Ballet performance of *The Sleeping Beauty* in New York. Photograph by Judy Cameron.

I recall his first *La Bayadère* in London, when he danced the role of Solor. This role demands aerial jumps, corkscrew turns, and every manner of beaten steps, and Nureyev carried them off with majesterial ease. *La Bayadère* is a ballet that makes no provision for anything less than the superlative. It is like crossing Niagara Falls on a tight-rope—you do it or you don't. The famous series of double assemblés en tournant were remarkable; Nureyev seemed to have adopted the Vasiliev step of a turn in attitude. On the first night he had not adopted it quite firmly enough, and his variation had to be brought to a hasty and premature end. But this fault was not repeated in subsequent performances when he danced with

With Merle Park in Nureyev's staging of *La Bayadère* for the Royal Ballet, 1963.
Photograph by Zoe Dominic.

In *La Bayadère*. Photograph by Judy Cameron.

impeccable virtuosity and stylishness. There was a single-mindedness about Nureyev's performance that in itself would be impressive. When he ran on to the stage, he ran with such intensity of purpose that his whole being seemed to be concentrated into the act. There was a most remarkable intensity about his stage personality. He electrified the audience before he even started to dance. There were moments when his actual dancing seemed to be a gratuitous bonus, but what a bonus it had become! His earlier untidiness had been virtually eliminated, and although he sometimes overreached himself through sheer daring, most of his work kept within the bounds of pure classicism.

Nureyev's first performance in *Les Sylphides* took place in London on May 3, 1962. It was a Gala program in which he partnered Yvette Chauviré. It seemed at the time that Chauviré shaded her dancing of the Prelude with a little too much expression, making it an overly-mannered performance. Here, too, she failed to show any noticeable rapport with her partner.

The choreographer of *Les Sylphides,* Michel Fokine, had a flexible, even changeable, mind. The male solo in *Les Sylphides,* introduced to the West by the Diaghilev Ballet and Nijinsky, is to the Mazurka in C Major, op. 67, no. 3. This is the version danced by most Western companies. However, subsequently in Russia, Fokine offered an alternative male solo danced to the Mazurka in C Major, op. 33, no. 3, and this is the version still danced by the Kirov Ballet. Nowadays Baryshnikov has inserted it into his American Ballet Theatre production. It was this rare version, with its grave elegance so suited to the young romantic dancer, that Nureyev chose for Covent Garden. It was, as it happened, a Western premiere.

Nureyev's haunted poet proved as effective as one might have expected, and his aerial dancing had a touch of genius. Male dancers in *Les Sylphides* are a select breed, and Nureyev was undoubtedly in their first rank. His elevation had a vital quality of daring, his *port de bras* a sensuous grace, his static poses a definition and significance that dominate the memory. He looked like a man who sees visions. Possibly he overplayed the romantic strain, and occasionally he allowed the outline of his dancing to become blurred. Yet there was always a wayward streak of genius in everything he did.

When Fonteyn later danced with him on November 6, 1962, in *Les Sylphides,* I would write:

"This performance by Fonteyn and Nureyev deserved to become legendary. Nureyev danced with solemn deliberation as if he was weighing the advisability of every step. The lean face and long hair looked just right. Here was a man to sit on gravestones and talk of love and mortality. This, I was reminded, is French romanticism seen through Russian eyes, and as a result is very serious and just a little mad.

"I feel that Nureyev is the only male dancer I have seen who presents the Poet as Fokine imagined him. He gives the appearance of complete solitude, of someone searching for inspiration or an ideal. The Sylphs are merely figments of his imagination, something which inspire him for a brief moment. He is not in love with them, so this air of apartness, of detachment, which some people criticized, is justified. The key to Nureyev's interpretation is in his face which seems always as though he expects to find in moonbeams what he is searching for. Nureyev has a face a sculptor would delight in and to which no amount of jostling adjectives can do justice."

It may have been that face that the great Diaghilev ballerina, Tamara Karsavina, had in

With Yvette Chauviré in Michel Fokine's *Les Sylphides,* Royal Ballet, 1962.
Photograph by Central Press Photos, Ltd.

mind, when she was asked whether Nureyev's power of projection was as great as Nijinsky's. She replied, "I, who have seen both, can honestly say it is. It seems to me that Nureyev's range is wider because of the mobility of his face in dramatics."

During this first phase of performing in the West, Nureyev essayed none of the master-pieces of the Diaghilev repertory, *Les Sylphides* and *Petrushka* aside. That area of dance is, of course, totally alien to the ruling aesthetic of contemporary Soviet ballet.

Certainly in Soviet Russia there is a version of *Les Sylphides,* still known by its pre-Diaghilev title of *Chopiniana,* which Nureyev had danced at the Kirov. Yet for the most part the heritage of Diaghilev, and of course Michel Fokine, its principal choreographer in the Diaghilev company's first days, is either unknown in Russia or preserved in only very corrupt and corrupted versions. This was obviously a matter of considerable interest to Nureyev when he came to the West. Also, this repertory was, to a large extent, based on the Russian dancer Vaslav Nijinsky at the beginning of the century, and right from the begin-ning of his career Nureyev found himself being compared with Nijinsky. Comparison between the two, the intermingling of their legend, intrigued Nureyev, who always seems to have had a certain ambivalent fascination for his great predecessor.

One can imagine when Nureyev was a young man, growing up in the Kirov studios, how he must have looked at the photographs of this strange Slavic figure in the Kirov's theater museum. He must have heard the background of murmurs of people who actually had seen Nijinsky dance at the beginning of the century, that here was at last a successor. And when he came to Western Europe, he was immediately hailed, as the true and only inheritor of a crown that very few people had ever seen.

The curious thing is how brief Nijinsky's career was in the West, and how compara-tively few people actually saw him dance. He danced comparatively rarely in New York and London, for example, and few people could have seen both dancers at their peak. One such person was the British critic and historian, C. W. Beaumont, and I remember asking him whether he thought there was any similarity between Nijinsky and Nureyev. He said he thought there was, and then suggested:..."those seemingly feline, asexual, and in some ways orientally exotic qualities which combined both spirituality with sensuousness."

Over the years Nureyev has danced many of Nijinsky's most famous roles. These include not only the Poet in *Les Sylphides,* but also Petrushka in *Petrushka,* the Spectre in *Le Spectre de la Rose,* the Golden Slave in *Schéhérazade,* and, of course, the Faun in Nijinsky's own ballet *L'Après-Midi d'un Faune.*

In all these portrayals he has worked conscientiously to achieve accuracy as well as period flavor. His performance as Petrushka is an excellent case in point. He was originally taught the role by Diaghilev's régisseurs, Lubov Tchernicheva and Serge Grigorieff. When he first danced it with the Royal Ballet at Covent Garden in 1963, I noted how the Benois/Stravinsky/Fokine puppet-hero could trace his ancestry from *commedia dell'arte* to fairground. Alexandre Benois, the original librettist, suggested that Petrushka should be taken as "the personification of the spiritual and suffering side of humanity—or shall we call it the poetical principle?" It is just this "poetical principle" that Nureyev so adeptly caught. This was a puppet of more sawdust than most. His glazed eyes and shambling manner, his constant note of terror, the thin intensity of his love, all contribute to a Petrushka of suffering rather than anger—a Petrushka more Russian and more instinctively authentic than we were accustomed to.

As a result, the pathetic, suffering Petrushka of Fokine's original intention came back into its own. Nureyev's performance was quite moving. His loosely hung puppet body seemed racked with anguish, his eyes stared purposelessly in front of him. The imploring agony of his breath was resigned, even the final mocking gestures of Petrushka's ghost took on a withdrawn and wanly ironic air.

Nureyev has continued to develop his portrayal of the puppet, until now it does very much have the impact and effect of all those descriptions of Nijinsky in this role. His eyes do glitter like black beads, his lopsided face looks washed out and blank with the pathos and poignancy of a clown out of joint, and his arms have that ramshackle articulation of a puppet still remembering his strings.

Both *Le Spectre de la Rose* and *Schéhérazade* he shied away from for many years, not dancing them until 1978 when he was already forty. He performed them for the first time in New York during the season at the Metropolitan Opera House with London Festival Ballet. And he gave them both on the same program, throwing in a debut in Bournonville's *Conservatoire* for good measure.

Both roles had been obviously subjected to considerable study. They gave the impression that Nureyev had read every word he could find about how Nijinsky danced, and somehow took this background into his muscles. Very few dancers have portrayed the sensuous yet ethereal spirit that the poet Vaudoyer first conceived in his libretto for *Le Spectre* and which Fokine embodied in the choreography. In this Beriosoff staging, Nureyev made wonderful use of the weaving, oriental *ports de bras*—those tendril-like arm movements, like art-nouveau traceries—the big leaps, the delicate beaten steps, and, of course, the famous arabesque penchée against the chair. He was a spirit, a poem, an image never quite lost—not so young as Nijinsky, to be sure, and without the melting grace of transient youth seen in the photographs—but everywhere else, alive with his own, always imperious personality. He was a rose with a difference, one with all the style to recall that marvelous Cocteau poster of Nijinsky in the very role.

Schéhérazade has a different and more difficult story. The ballet itself has dated in a way that *Le Spectre de la Rose* has not. Its elephantine harem antics, its Arabian nights aroma and ornate decorations, make it a ballet difficult for modern audiences to accept. It would perhaps be more popular in Russia. Yet somehow, more than any other dancer who has portrayed the Golden Slave in recent times, Nureyev—moving like an animal in heat, savoring freedom and sensuality—did succeed in making one understand what it was that transfixed audiences in Paris and London when Nijinsky danced it.

Hardly anyone risks Nijinsky's *Faune* now, although it is the only remnant of his startling choreography that remains to us. Since the War, I have seen it in Europe with Jean Babilée—who challenged but did not match Nureyev—as well as in a bizarre solo version with Serge Lifar. The present version derives from the repertory of the Ballet Rambert which has maintained it for years. Although history has long overtaken the ballet's suggestion of scandal, its two-dimensional frieze-like choreography, its suggestion of erotic rites and wall paintings, still has potency. Nureyev marvelously caught all those hard-edged poses and postures imprinted on our minds from the Nijinsky photographs. There was perhaps as much artistry in this remarkable evocation of the Nijinsky image as there was in the loving and lovely reconstruction of the set and costumes.

One can understand in some respects why Nureyev identifies so closely with Nijinsky— it is surely not simply that they came out of the same school and made much the same journey to the West. Admittedly, Nureyev's was more sensational, but their careers were essentially very similar. Both were the darlings of their contemporary publics, both were associated with a great ballerina: Nijinsky with Tamara Karsavina, and Nureyev with Margot Fonteyn, Karsavina's pupil. Also, both of them in any psychological sense must be regarded as loners. They are typical of the twentieth century artist as outcast, the twentieth century artist as lonely man. Both seem to have had strong religious impulses, both seem to have been men attracted to and repelled by Russia, and both, perhaps most of all, had an almost supernatural concern for the Dance itself. Both men were intensely driven and intensely dedicated. Nureyev was obviously the better equipped to deal with his life. When he came to the West, he in a very real sense became Western. Nijinsky, it seems never did. Nijinsky faced mental problems that eventually overthrew him. But they both had the same pressures and similar geniuses. Both of them were not merely dancers but very important creative artists.

Nureyev's creative career has had a far longer span, he has also moved with much more care and delicacy in pacing his creative abilities so that they can keep pace with his knowledge of his craftsmanship.

There has been little in the rest of the Diaghilev repertory that had either tempted

Nureyev or has come Nureyev's way. For example, one would have enjoyed seeing him as the Hussar in Léonide Massine's *Le Beau Danube*, but in fact he has never danced in a Massine ballet, which, given the circumstances, is rather odd. It might have been fun to have seen him as the Miller in *The Three Cornered Hat*, or even as the Peruvian Traveler in *Gaité Parisienne*. It is odd that his talent for the grotesque and the humorous has very rarely been exploited either by choreographers or by himself. Massine might have brought out something of that fantastic comic quality that lurks behind so many of Nureyev's classic roles—in his Romeo for example, or in the more overt comedy of Colas in Ashton's *La Fille Mal Gardée* and Franz in Erik Bruhn's version of *Coppélia*. Even more surprising is the fact that he has not danced any original ballet by Bronislava Nijinska, in whom one would have expected him to find a perfect choreographer. However, not many of Nijinska's ballets have survived, and one could hardly envisage him in *Les Noces*. Nevertheless, it would have been fun to have seen him—and perhaps it will be fun one day to see him—in the central role of *Les Biches*, and at one time it might have been interesting—to say the least—to see him as the acrobatic Le Gosse created for Anton Dolin in Nijinska's *Le Train Bleu*.

Since the early days at Covent Garden Nureyev's career has gone far and wide. He has concentrated in many areas, yet, in a sense, it is his work in the classic ballet which shows the purest vein of his genius.

Ballet acting is never as complex as stage acting; no one is going to be able to play Hamlet in a ballet with the same sort of intellectual insight that an actor would bring to the Shakespearean role. Although ballet acting does indeed lack this sort of cerebral brilliance, with its mixture of emotion and intellect, it does at the same time have an almost instinctive awareness, a much more basic awareness of what the character is really about. If you cannot convey a character in words, then your very gestures, every tiny movement, every glance of the eyes, every curl of the lips, has to be expressive in a different, a more imaginative fashion. The dramatic actor produces a portrait; the dance actor produces a symbol. And between the two there is, of course, a vast difference. So it is foolish to try to compare the two arts.

It was in the acute manner with which Nureyev was able to produce ballet acting that something of his greatness, something of his unique quality, first emerged. Here was not just a man who jumped higher, moved faster, did any number of technical feats that his large public began to admire. Here was a man who was important simply because he was introducing a new kind of characterization to our stage.

Nureyev was one of the dancers who tried to show the difference between a conventional hero and a human being. He was not the only dancer of that time to try to make the prince's role rather less pallid, to give it some kind of heart, some semblance of human nature. The great Danish dancer, Erik Bruhn, a colleague and friend of Nureyev's, and a considerable influence on Nureyev's style, was also attempting the same transference.

I think Bruhn's ability to act confirmed Nureyev in his concept that dancing was not just a question of going through steps, that it was much more a question of presenting a person on the stage. It is interesting that Bruhn, a superb technician, admired and envied Nureyev's crowd-pleasing, crowd-cheering qualities, his enormous jump, his romantic manner which embraced the entire audience with one sweep. These were things that Bruhn never had. What Bruhn did have was immaculate technique. He was a perfectionist, and equally important, he had the ability which Nureyev soon acquired to become a person on stage.

When, for example, Bruhn danced Don José in Petit's *Carmen*—the ballet is itself trivial—Bruhn made Don José into a person of such compelling power that even when he wiped the soap off his razor on a curtain, suddenly the gesture became the person. Most people will say that Nureyev acquired Bruhn's interest in technique; I would say he acquired Bruhn's ability to identify himself totally with a role without dancing.

One of the great things Bruhn did was in a ballet called *A Folk Tale* by Bournonville, in which he played Ove, a role with no dancing in it at all, requiring him only to portray a kind of peasant prince, a role infused with something of Hans Christian Andersen's spirit of gentility. Bruhn did it all with noble elegance, without dancing, and even though I doubt that Nureyev saw him in it, it was the nature of the Danish master's approach that had, I think, so great an influence on the young Russian. Certainly it was a major influence on the superb James that Nureyev danced in *La Sylphide* with the National Ballet of Canada during its 1973 New York engagement. Bruhn's version of the Bournonville choreography exhibited a special esprit and understanding, and Nureyev adopted that literally like a native, giving us a braw Highlander who was also the epitome of balletic Romanticism—wild-eyed, yet classically perfect.

I think it was the Stanislavsky schooling at the Kirov that made Nureyev very receptive to acting. Even when he arrived in the West he was a very good actor. I always remember the first role that was created for him in the West, Scriabin's *Poème Tragique*, by Ashton. It was incredibly moving, poignant. It had an image of reality, the pressure of reality, the imprint of reality. He was at the back of the stage and started by running down stage, holding his hand up in a gesture of both defiance and despair at the same time; and it was totally there, it was there on stage, it was there in your heart, it was there for all time. He danced it only once in his life.

Nureyev's quest for credibility in the role he was playing had obviously started in Russia. Yet it was only when he came to the West that his quest became almost a mission.

You could see it happening almost from performance to performance. When he first danced Albrecht to Margot Fonteyn's Giselle at Covent Garden in 1962, it was his actual performance that was so stunning, and, of course, that remarkably flamboyant theatrical presence that always hung around his every stage gesture. He had already danced most of the classic roles in Soviet Russia, where—despite the limitations imposed on every young Soviet artist—he had been given enormous opportunities. He had been entrusted with the roles of Albrecht in *Giselle*, Prince Florimund in *The Sleeping Beauty*, Basilio in *Don Quixote*. Yet this was not enough. He felt constricted. He was never given the opportunity to create new roles.

He saw foreign companies like the New York City Ballet on a Russian tour, and a major influence on his thinking came from Balanchine's *The Four Temperaments*. All of this gave him a new insight, a new yearning, to make something different, something remote from the normal Soviet pattern of dance. He was not content merely to repeat what he had been taught in class, not content simply to improve on the technical perfections of the past. He very soon felt that Soviet ballet was something of a polishing process, something that had more to do with the exposure of the past rather than the exploration of the future. For someone of Nureyev's character and ability, this simply was not enough. It was this special need and spirit, more than anything else, that prompted his jump to the West.

When he found himself in the West, he found himself in a world in many ways different, in many ways confusing. He was expecting to find an entirely new world of creative ferment. In a way he did, and in a way he didn't. His first experience of new choreography, that solo created by Ashton, did seem to immortalize his special flight to the West and his special position as an artistic and social rebel.

It was this need for creation, this need to work with choreographers in the West that was of prime importance to the young artist. Nureyev could sense, even as a young man, the limitations of Soviet Art. He knew that it was not sufficient merely to obey party doctrine, merely to accept preconditioned artistic values. He knew that he had to find some new artistic freedom for himself and to work with that for the rest of his life. Ironically, when he first joined Britain's Royal Ballet, he danced only Princes, and the irony must have occurred to him of jumping over the iron curtain, of travelling so many miles to eventually end up doing the same roles he would have been doing in Soviet Russia.

He made it clear that he wished to be integrated into the Royal Ballet, and as a result, he soon started to appear in repertory ballets. I recall him particularly in two ballets of this

In Michel Fokine's *Prince Igor* at a Royal Ballet Gala, 1965. Photograph from the Theatre Museum, Houston Rogers Collection (Victoria and Albert Museum, London).

In *Prince Igor*, Royal Ballet. Photograph by Central Press Photos, Ltd.

period, Kenneth MacMillan's *Diversions* and John Cranko's *Antigone*. The MacMillan work was a purely plotless ballet, and it was the first time that Covent Garden had seen Nureyev in any role that did not involve the presentation of a character. The contrast between these two ballets was enormous. MacMillan had created, to music by Arthur Bliss, a plotless work that was bland and simple, yet Nureyev invested it with his own particular power and presence. He showed a fluent style, and, much more, a complete command of the elemental nature of such plotless dancing. For someone who had never had any experience of this kind of role in Russia, it was perhaps a more notable achievement than it appeared on the surface. He was totally able to subjugate his personality to the demands of the role, and those demands were quite different from anything he had previously encountered. In a way it was the beginning of his baptism in the West.

In *Antigone*, Cranko made a dramatic work full of fire and fury—in some ways a little empty—but with sharply defined characterizations. Nureyev brought precisely the same quality of conviction to this that he did to MacMillan's *Diversions*. In both ballets he was perfectly himself, bridging the gap between acting and being. The role of Etiocles in *Antigone* was something of a departure. However, it was not quite the same as *Diversions*. With *Antigone* he was on familiar ground, for this was the first time in the West that he had tackled a

118   With David Drew and Svetlana Beriosova in John Cranko's *Antigone*, Royal Ballet, 1962. Photograph by Anthony Crickmay.

purely demi-charactère role. In *Diversions* he looked rather an exotic odd-man out. Nureyev danced with a mixture of romantic ardor and sulky heroism that needed a lot of toning down for the true-blue British reticence. Yet his willingness to make these excursions into the unfamiliar was, in itself, splendid for the man and valuable for the company.

Cranko had given the two warring brothers in *Antigone* a great amount of athletic choreography, combined with a firm sense of characterization. In fact, this was an extension of the kind of ballets that Nureyev had been used to in Russia. He took to the Cranko conception of a hero as naturally as duck to water or swan to lake. In Nureyev's first appearance in *Antigone*, a man in black and white tights swept onto the stage in high, exultant leaps. Someone who had been taken to see Nureyev for the first time murmured appreciatively to a colleague of mine: "He's very good, isn't he?" He was very good, but he wasn't Nureyev; he was David Drew as Polynices. Nureyev was dancing, and dancing excellently, the rather less sensational role of Etiocles. For the first time in his career Nureyev was appearing *with* the Royal Ballet, rather than having the Royal Ballet as his backcloth. It was a milestone passed. Here he was subjugating himself to the team, and at the end, one felt like clapping him all the way back to the pavilion. What was particularly interesting about Nureyev in *Antigone* was the manner in which he absorbed the character. As one of Thebes'

With Lynn Seymour and Christopher Gable in Kenneth MacMillan's *Images of Love,* Royal Ballet, 1963. Photograph by Anthony Crickmay.

119

fratricidal brothers, he had a purring quality of menace. Like Tybalt, he was a King of Cats.

Soon after he appeared in *Diversions* and in *Antigone,* he also danced in Ashton's masterpiece *Symphonic Variations.* Although he danced the role in London only one time, Nureyev was among the finest interpreters of the ballet. When he danced it, he was suffering from a fever, but it did not seem to matter. He danced this fluent, fluid Ashton choreography with remarkable authority and power. This was an indication of how he was going to make his own imprint on the choreography of the West. The Russian firebird played up and played the game superbly. Never once stepping out of line, he nevertheless managed to add a personal touch of glamour to his dancing that added to the ballet's effectiveness. His free almost rhapsodic arm movements had a specifically Russian kind of eloquence that seemed out of place in the colder climate of this most British of all ballets. Yet, this apart, he fitted perfectly into the ensemble. He did have a quite different approach to plotless choreography from that of his British colleagues. Partly I suspect this lay in his approach to the music, but even more in his approach to the whole *idea* of giving a performance. He apparently felt impelled to interpret the music in overtly emotional as well as purely physical terms. Where British dancers took an objective view of the music, letting their limbs speak for them as it were, Nureyev's approach was altogether more subjective. He interpreted music, bringing to it the Romantic air of a poet seeing visions. What could look affected, with him seemed natural, and this distinctive touch of poetry, far from disturbing the ballet's balance, added to its interest.

His face mirrored his dancing, and there was a strong similarity here to the poetic languors he brought to *Les Sylphides.* Something of this added emotional dimension seemed to transfer itself to Fonteyn. Her dancing here was always poised and womanly, but now she added a certain rapt quality that, to be fanciful perhaps, had a happy air of sanctity about it. Her impressive delicacy had thawed into positive serenity.

During this period of Nureyev's first adventures in what might be called the plotless ballets of the West, he became a completely blank sheet. In Russia he had become accustomed to the special circumstances of interpretation. He had understood the certain roles of prince. He had understood the certain roles of heroism, the certain positions of a Soviet hero. But here in the West he suddenly found himself faced with a new kind of interpretation that did not depend upon the non-essentials of specific drama, rather, as with Ashton's *Symphonic Variations,* upon a new kind of expressiveness derived in large part from simple dance patterns of a body in space. This was something that Nureyev had not had to face in Russia. He suddenly found himself, for the first time, faced with the simple expression of himself quite apart from any character. This was to prove of paramount importance to him in future years.

One of the testing times was with Kenneth MacMillan's *Romeo and Juliet*. This was a ballet that MacMillan created not for Rudolf Nureyev and his partner Margot Fonteyn, but for Christopher Gable and Lynn Seymour. Yet the ballet seemed to fit Nureyev like a glove, as it did Fonteyn. They both swept into the MacMillan choreography like young lovers at their first passion. Nureyev had never previously had choreography that was so much himself, so much his appreciation of the world. To an extent, Romeo, whether it was created for him or not, marked a new definition of his career in the West. It was the part that offered him something radically different. It presented him neither as an abstract hero nor as one of the puppet princes, but quite simply as a human being. At the time such a possibility meant a great deal to Nureyev. It was a marvelous role. MacMillan had taken a great deal from John Cranko's earlier realization of the Prokofiev score. On the other hand, MacMillan was able to give certain connotations to the ballet which were unique. Also with the help of Nicholas Georgiadis, MacMillan gave the Prokofiev *Romeo and Juliet* a new vitality and special quality. For many people this Royal Ballet *Romeo and Juliet* became the standard version. Among the major reasons for this were the performances of Rudolf Nureyev and Margot Fonteyn.

With Kenneth MacMillan, John Hart, and Margot Fonteyn at a rehearsal of *Romeo and Juliet*. Photograph by Reg Wilson/Camera Press Ltd.

The partnership of Fonteyn and Nureyev is something that must be investigated as well as wondered at. Fonteyn was many years Nureyev's senior, and she was a dancer who consistently improved. It is difficult to understand Nureyev without understanding Fonteyn. When Nureyev arrived, she had reached a stage in her career to which only retirement could have expressed a suitable tribute. Given the opportunity to dance with Nureyev, the retirement receded into the far distance. Somehow she found in Nureyev a new vitality, life, and career.

The Fonteyn-Nureyev partnership is one of those destined to be remembered in history as one of the greatest ballet partnerships. Most of the historic partnerships are not all that consistent. One talks of Anna Pavlova and Vaslav Nijinsky, but in fact they only danced together on very few occasions. One can talk about Karsavina and Nijinsky, but even they, although rather more consistent, did not dance together that much. One talks of later partnerships—Alicia Markova and Anton Dolin, Alexandra Danilova and Frederic Franklin—all those people who really were important ballet teams in the West. Fonteyn herself had had many partners. She started with Robert Helpmann, who in fact was, in her time, more important to her company, the emerging Vic-Wells, later to become the Royal Ballet, than she was herself. For most of her early career, when she was partnered by Helpmann, it was not she who was the major artist; it was Helpmann. He sold the tickets, not Fonteyn. Helpmann was never a very strong dancer, but as an actor he was unequalled, and he was a very good partner.

Later Fonteyn had other partners. She had an enormously important partnership with Michael Somes, a major collaboration in British ballet. When Somes started to partner her, an entirely new aspect of Fonteyn emerged. She became freer, more eloquent, and, most of all, more technically at ease. She was always a dancer who developed technically as the years went on. Indeed, she developed quite unexpectedly. One would never have expected Fonteyn to have been so fantastic in 1956 if one had seen her in 1946 when she first opened the Royal Opera House, Covent Garden, at the Royal Gala. This was an almost unexpected benefit. Fonteyn kept on getting better. You could never calculate how much better she was going to get. When she first emerged as a child, you saw that she was going to be *that* good. But then as she got older she certainly became *that* good, and then she became *that* much better. There are very few dancers who have improved consistently, kept their art in line with their talent, and kept their possibility in line with their physical aptitude to the degree that Margot Fonteyn has. She has been a wonder of the Western world. And so it was no accident, and certainly no distress to either of them, that Fonteyn and Nureyev found their careers inextricably allied.

With Georgina Parkinson in Kenneth MacMillan's *Romeo and Juliet*, Royal Ballet 1965. Photograph by Mike Davis Studios, Ltd.

When you think of Nureyev as an artist, you have to think of Fonteyn. The odd thing was that Fonteyn was already an artist in what might have been considered her fallow years, years in which she would have gone through her past with sympathy, recognized her failings, and slipped into retirement will all the graciousness that her ballerinadom would have bestowed. Suddenly in the Indian summer of her career, Nureyev appeared. It was a shattering career experience for her. For him, it was something totally new.

I was puzzled, but there she was. . . I considered her without technique, yet she was doing technical things. . .and me, taught the best technique. . .(that was the idea I guess every other Russian dancer who comes to the West will think that way, exactly). How is it possible that she without technique was doing technical things, and I am with technique and not always there. . .so there I created from my experience, from the best school somehow. . . and mostly I'd do what I want to do, she'd let me rehearse without confrontation but then we tried out with the mirror, she would look and see. . .when she was the better, I would surrender. . .

Together they became the biggest, most important dance combination the world has known, and possibly ever will know. Fonteyn and Nureyev—for about ten years theirs was a patent to dance without equal. Together they made theatrical magic. Even apart they carried the trails of their previous glory. But it was when they were together that everything worked out, that the entire dance world understood that this was a very special experience.

All over Europe and the United States, Fonteyn and Nureyev became a team of dancers that could offer a special individuality of experience. One of the reasons why dance today is so popular is undoubtedly due to efforts of Fonteyn and Nureyev since they made dance available to so many people. They did the kind of task that Anna Pavlova and Mikhail Mordkin had in the past performed. But they were performing in an era of mass media in an arena when the dance was ready for some incredible explosion of understanding. It is no accident that dance in the United States and all over the world exploded just at the time that Fonteyn and Nureyev made their major tours and brought dance to a level that the entire world could comprehend. They were news in a way that no other dancers had ever been news before. It was time when artistry was almost of secondary importance to charisma. Nureyev and Fonteyn showed the world a kind of charisma that had been lacking in dance for many, many years.

The culmination of the partnership of Fonteyn and Nureyev, and in a way its memorial, will always be Frederick Ashton's ballet *Marguerite and Armand*. This was a ballet in one act which had music by Franz Liszt, originally orchestrated by Humphrey Searle, and scenery and costumes by Cecil Beaton. It was a message to the world of the special dance

As Romeo. Photograph by Louis Péres.

style of these two great romantic artists. Many years before, Tamara Karsavina and Vaslav Nijinsky had, with the help of Michel Fokine, given us *Le Spectre de la Rose*. *Marguerite and Armand* was for Fonteyn and Nureyev their *Spectre de la Rose*. This was something absolutely unexpected. It had its first performance on March 12, 1963 at Covent Garden. In the same year, on May 1, the same dancers gave the ballet's New York premiere at the Metropolitan Opera House.

To an extent this version of the Dumas story of *The Lady of the Camellias* must seem oddly familiar. It was not the first time that this story had been adapted for ballet. Versions had already been given by such choreographers as Anton Dolin and John Taras. However, it was Ashton's inspiration that made this ballet work. And Ashton's inspiration was based totally upon these two remarkable dancers. Here he saw a vehicle for two of the greatest dancers who had ever entered his range. Here were Fonteyn and Nureyev. Here was the opportunity to create a work that would make them memorable for all time. Ashton presented his work with great simplicity and, yet, an enduring force.

When it was first produced at Covent Garden, many of the criticisms were lukewarm. Ashton works have a tendency to be difficult to accept at first seeing. They almost seem too easy, too fluent, too urbane. It takes a critic some time to understand the depth charge of passion that is at the basis of almost all of Ashton's work. This depth charge has never been more apparent, never more explosive, than it was in *Marguerite and Armand*.

The tension of the first night was considerable. There had been a lot of difficulties facing the ballet in its early production stages, and no one quite knew what to expect. It had so much of the hoopla of public relations around it, and it was a work that no one expected to turn out in any manner other than a vehicle for its two distinguished, indeed superstar, leading artists. What did emerge that March night at Covent Garden was remarkable. Writing about it the following morning in the London Times, I found myself saying: "The swiftness of the ballet gives it a hallucinatory quality, a sense of flying passion, of a tragedy fitfully illuminated by flashes of Keats' 'spangly doom'. Here is the true romantic agony distilled into a brief ballet, far more pungent in its effect than any *Giselle*."

It exploded on the world and it exploded expectedly. It was precisely what people were expecting of this wild Lisztian romance between Fonteyn and Nureyev. Yet, it was so much better than most people were prepared to recognize. *Marguerite and Armand* is the major work for Fonteyn and Nureyev, an absolute signature piece, the one work that was created for them in absolute toto and the one that showed both of them at their absolute best. They have revived it for one another often, and it still works even now. It is a ballet that exploits both their technique and their emotional bases. No choreographer had probed so deeply into their personalities before. *Marguerite and Armand* took both dancers to the pinnacle of their

With Cecil Beaton and Frederick Ashton at a rehearsal of *Marguerite and Armand,* during the filming of *I Am a Dancer,* 1972. Photograph by Zoë Dominic.

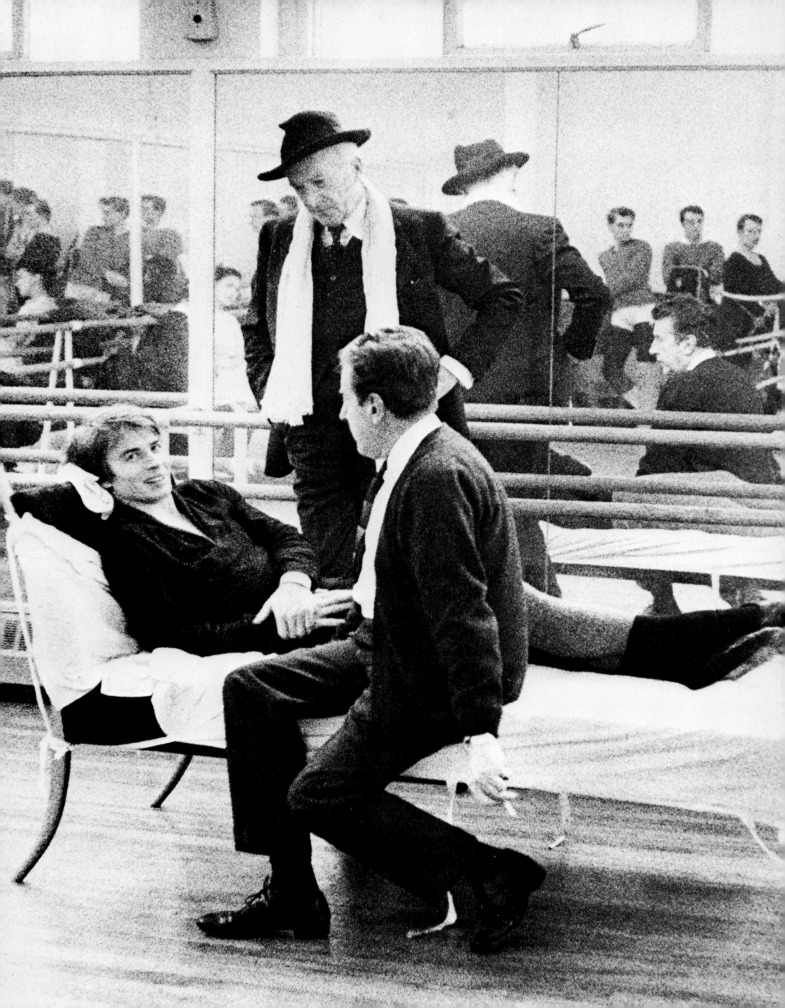

128   With Margot Fonteyn and Frederick Ashton. Photograph from the Theatre Museum, Houston
Rogers Collection (Victoria and Albert Museum, London).

skills. Nureyev was absolutely brilliant. He was not simply brilliant in a way of a dancer, although certainly on that night long ago he did dance with such brilliance, such sheer technical élan that you wondered whether anyone had quite had that fire, even that expertise, ever before. Maybe, but you could never be sure.

Yet what was interesting about both Fonteyn and Nureyev in this ballet was their total involvement with the image of romanticism. For both of them this was an experiment in time. Both of them had been used to using the paraphernalia of ballet, its tricks and its starts, its nonsense and its flamboyances. What was truly important about *Marguerite and Armand* was the manner in which Frederick Ashton made both his dancers part of a plan, part of a dramatic vision of a way of life, a way of love, and an excursion into nineteenth century European literature. It was a fascinatingly literary ballet. Almost everything about it was redolent of books.

Although it was a literary ballet and intended to be so, it still had a most remarkable concept of the dancer as a dancer. In every moment of the work both of these very great dancers—then at the height of their fame, were also at the height of their particular interpretative genius. These roles simply worked: Fonteyn, the courtesan, shattered with fears of love, her entire body ravaged with certain understanding of mortality; Nureyev, a young man, a poet intent on creating the image of himself in a new world. He finds this remarkable courtesan, beautiful, aware, witty, and yet tragically dying. The two were made for one another. Ashton realized it. Ashton made the ballet about Marguerite and Armand that will surely be definitive.

This is one of the great classic love stories of our time. Yet all of its many realizations have never had such a perfect interpretation as Margot Fonteyn and Rudolf Nureyev were able to offer. It was partly a matter of age, partly of achievement, a matter quite simply that Ashton created a choreographic fabric completely to their abilities and talents, even more to their personalities. For example, imagine Nureyev's dance of simple triumph when he was going off to town little knowing that he will not find Marguerite there when he returns. It is a masterpiece of compression, concision, and choreographic understanding. Ashton was totally aware of the story, totally aware of the way he was working with his dancers, and totally aware of the work he was going to give to the world.

Of course Ashton had worked with Fonteyn from her beginning in the thirties. Fonteyn was certainly a known factor. Nureyev was something different, completely different. He was a figure thrown into the British ballet world almost by circumstance, yet dominating almost by right. It was a difficult time, and Ashton had to evaluate many questions and many answers. With *Marguerite and Armand,* however, Ashton produced a work that had simple beauty, maintained the special ethos of those particular dancers, and immortalized them.

Marguerite and Armand is a lovely ballet. When it first emerged most people did not understand what they were seeing. They thought they were seeing a vehicle, and in fact they were seeing a Rolls-Royce. By its very simplicity, it takes one's breath away. Equally by simplicity, it makes one nervous of having been sold. It is a ballet that appeals to all people, all the time.

I remember originally the work was postponed because of an injury. I also recall suggesting to Ashton that he should not hold up the ballet for Fonteyn and Nureyev, but that he

With Margot Fonteyn in *Marguerite and Armand*. Photograph from the Theatre Museum, Houston Rogers Collection (Victoria and Albert Museum, London).

The final scene in *Marguerite and Armand*. Photograph by Judy Cameron.

should go ahead with Irina Baronova—a great dancer of the Ballets Russes of approximately Fonteyn's generation—and a young dancer, Christopher Gable. It would have been a sensation, particularly to move the premiere away from Fonteyn and Nureyev and give it to other dancers. Ashton would hear nothing of it, and I must say that Ashton was right.

No one other than Fonteyn and Nureyev has ever danced *Marguerite and Armand.* Every other major ballet has been sometimes corrupted, sometimes enhanced by other dancers, but never ignored by other dancers. Here is a work that seems to be unique to these two dancers. It may be that Ashton saw them in these two particular roles, and said: "This is what I want my ballet to be, and nothing else." You could see that when you saw Fonteyn and Nureyev dance *Marguerite and Armand.* Fonteyn and Nureyev *are* Marguerite and Armand; Ashton's choreography is their choreography. To an extent unusual even in Ashton, the ballet has been based on its dancers so that their style is embedded right in the heart of the choreography. This hectic choreography with all its plunges and its grapplings, still bears traces of classic elegance; but it is far wilder than anything Ashton has created before. Nureyev seems to have prompted the same revolution in Ashton that he earlier prompted in Fonteyn.

Even to a greater extent than Fonteyn's Marguerite, Armand is derived from Nureyev. Even on his first entrance, he strikes a pose from *Le Corsaire,* and time and time again the ballet practically quotes him. But such is Ashton's wizardry that he has borrowed Nureyev's choreography, breathed over it, touched it up a little, and handed it back transfigured if not transformed.

Nureyev goes through *Marguerite and Armand* like a fiery arrow shot by destiny. His wild theatricality, the charge he can give the simplest pose or movement, the impact of his dancing, are used to telling effect. Nureyev's half-mocking smile, his abrupt authority, his savage despair—all these are Armand. It remains Nureyev's ballet. Here is an Armand of wild dreams, fierce authority and depths of feeling the choreographer can plumb but not fully chart. I can imagine the ballet without Fonteyn; but I find it impossible to envisage it without Nureyev.

With *Marguerite and Armand,* Fonteyn and Nureyev developed their curtain calls to the point and pattern of pure art. The flowers were thrown in earnest. Nureyev scooped some up as he went off. Dame Margot would sink low to the ground, lost in wonderment. As the frenzy escalated or at times diminished into a throb of unison clapping, the two stars took their calls together. Sometimes he grabbed a handful of the flowers and presented them to his lady. Given a single rose from her bouquet, he replied by catching her hand and kissing it violently, while the audience almost sighed at the wild, ardent beauty of it all.

The whole ritual acquired a certain immortality as the *Guinness Book of World Records* recorded after a Fonteyn and Nureyev performance in *Swan Lake* at the Vienna State Opera in October, 1964 that theirs was the greatest number of curtain calls ever received by ballet dancers—eighty-nine in fact. This record, to date unsurpassed, is featured in each updated edition.

There is no doubt that when Nureyev came to the West, he had been inspired to come by the presence of choreographers that he felt were superior to those then working in the Soviet Union. This was the prime reason for his so-called defection. In the West he has shown an incredible curiosity, a willingness to experiment—and to be experimented upon—almost beyond belief.

Nureyev never lost his hope there would be choreographers interested in his mind and in his body, challenged by that very special dramatic and classic style of his dancing, captivated by his romantic approach to the dance which has always been the basis of his art. He discovered many choreographers who indeed were eager and inspired to work with the fantastic possibilities he offered. The number has by now become legion. But some choreographers, perhaps the ones he most wanted, have been reluctant.

His first near rejection was from Frederick Ashton. Ashton was the choreographer—possibly more even than Balanchine—whom Nureyev most admired. Ashton, while a genius, was also a desultory genius. The great sadness of the relationship between Ashton and Nureyev has been that Ashton, perhaps simply through artistic inertia, has created so little for Nureyev. Their relationship has always been clouded by Ashton's reluctance to do the kind of work, at the pitch of intensity, that Nureyev demanded. He did, indeed, create Nureyev's first work in the West, the solo to Scriabin's *Poème Tragique*. Yet, after that, although Ashton admired Nureyev, liked him, and was always willing to work with him in certain areas, he never seemed prepared to put himself on the line and make Nureyev the instrument for his choreography in the way that a decade earlier he had with Margot Fonteyn.

This may have been due to Ashton's certain reluctance and certain nervousness about male technique. It must be remembered that Ashton developed in a style of choreography and a period of English ballet where the male technician was almost an unknown entity. Ashton was a very great choreographer, but his upbringing, which was similar to that of the Anglo-American choreographer, Antony Tudor, did not provide the experience in his youth of working with strong male dancers. As a result, it is quite possible that he was, to a certain degree, ill at ease, even nonplussed, by Nureyev's phenomenal technical facility, and his willingness to try anything twice. Ashton worked with him, but in a way that Nureyev could only believe was desultory. He wanted to work as much as possible, and over a long period of time Ashton had created only *Marguerite and Armand* for him. Although this is

going to become, in time, to the legend of Fonteyn and Nureyev, precisely what *Le Spectre de la Rose* is to the legend of Karsavina and Nijinsky, it was not the body of work that Nureyev needed. This was not why Nureyev jumped over that barrier at Le Bourget.

Frederick Ashton and I were very good friends and had mutual admiration. He said: "Rudka, let me rehearse you, let me prepare you in new ballets...you know in Russian school you learn it as it is not supposed to be"...and I said: I have no courage, I just can't yet, let me do this year the way I learned from Pushkin, from Kirov, from Sergeyev...the way it was passed on...then next year, I promise, I will do exactly as you wish it...so that went for many years...finally he gave up, and he took up on Anthony Dowell.

From Ashton, Nureyev moved to various other choreographers. He was not a dancer who felt instinctively that he had it in his muscles to release the genius of his own movement.

134   Curtain call at the conclusion of the Ashton Gala, London, July, 1970: Alexander Grant, Merle Park, Nureyev, Margot Fonteyn, John Lanchbery, John Hart, Sir Frederick Ashton. Photograph courtesy of the Royal Ballet Press office.

Nureyev seems always to have wanted to be directed. Curiously enough, if he knew something from his background, he could always develop that, yet he always had the need for—not exactly tuition, and hardly guidance—but the creative force to come to him from outside. Perhaps he will become his own choreographer. Certainly Martha Graham, a dancer and a dance personality with whom he has a great deal in common, discovered very early on that she had to create her own vocabulary, her own way of moving, and her own library of work. She had to become the creator for her own body.

To an extent Nureyev is a talent of that type. He had no concept of his own creative talent. He had been brought up within the rigid Kirov school, he had come from an underprivileged background in the Urals (imagine a Pioneer camp in Ufa), and he had none of the confidence that someone like Martha Graham brought to dance or, for that matter, to her own person.

Nureyev, by contrast, had been taught that he would have to be taught. It had always been part of his tradition that he was a dancer and not a choreographer. Ballet masters and choreographers were a race apart. *He* was a dancer. In this way he quite possibly not only underestimated his own creative talents but also supressed them. He wanted choreographers to work with him, and I have never yet heard of a choreographer who was dissatisfied with a Nureyev performance of his work. Now that is very rare indeed. He has worked with so many.

Nureyev's imagination, inquisitiveness, and cat-like ability to look into anything were obviously going to find outlets. As a result, over the years Nureyev has espoused, helped, and been both victim and instrument to almost every adventurous Western choreographer who came up and offered him a visiting card.

The results have been extraordinary. Nureyev has experimented in areas of choreography that he never had to, that his fans would certainly not have wanted him to, but that were absolutely essential to the fulfillment of himself. It would have been perfectly easy for him to have gone on dancing only *Swan Lake, Giselle* and all those other Russian and post-Russian extravaganzas for the rest of his life. He would have made more money. He might even have eased his muscles a little, not had to work at such intensity. But he would not have expanded his mind and have extended his heart and soul—which has been the entire message of Nureyev in the West, the reason for his flight, and the balance of his entire life as an artist.

Nureyev wants to experience everything. He has a genius that is continually questing, continually asking, continually trying to push itself into new areas of life and experience. He is an artist who is never content with yesterday's painting. What he wants, what he always wants, what he demands is some new challenge.

Probably the single greatest challenge Nureyev was to encounter in Western ballet—and the one that was never adequately resolved—was the challenge offered by the work of George Balanchine.

I think that one of the most curious relationships that Nureyev has had in the West has been his on-off, love-hate relationship with Balanchine. One would have expected Balanchine to have been the ideal choreographer for Nureyev. And I honestly believe that one of the reasons that Nureyev came to the West was his enormous admiration for Balanchine's work. When Nureyev suggested to Balanchine that he join the New York City Ballet, it soon became obvious as they talked about it that neither was for the other. There was no genuine connection between them; their aims and their artistic purposes were quite diverse. On the other hand, they both had a wary respect for themselves and a wary respect for the other.

After he had decided that Balanchine's company was not for him—and it was a mutual decision—Nureyev maintained an intense desire to dance in the Balanchine repertory. He has achieved this in many ways.

He has danced *The Prodigal Son, Agon, Theme and Variations, Rubies* and above all, he has danced *Apollo* with a mythic nobility that seems to capture that mixture of antiquity and modernism so essential to both the choreography and the Stravinsky score. In some respects you might think that he had courted the Balanchine repertory. Some companies have undoubtedly asked him, wooed him, to become part of a season by offering Balanchine roles he had not yet danced.

Nureyev has many things in common—surprisingly perhaps—with George Balanchine. Perhaps the first thing is their respect for what emerges from the orchestra pit.

Nureyev was determined to discover some range of dance outside of what he had been taught in Russia. At the same time—and this is very clear in his career—he was rigidly determined to retain what Russia and the Kirov school had given him. This is another of the ways in which he may best be compared with Balanchine, who was always intent on retaining his Kirov heritage. Always Balanchine's ballets refer back to Petipa, Ivanov, Gorsky, and his teachers, Lopukhov and Goleizovsky. And yet there was also in Balanchine this desire to experience the very wine of artistic freedom. And Nureyev, so many years later, was precisely the same. At the time of their meeting, it would have been quite impossible for Nureyev and Balanchine to have worked together.

Nureyev has a strong regard for himself as a star. This is not as egotistical as one might think. Nureyev's concept of himself as a star does not relate to any degree of vanity. It is much more a concept of being able to do what he wants when he wants to do it. It is a concept of artistic fulfillment.

...there is a constant fight against that image of being a star, superstar, whatever it means, I do not know...or whatever monstrous tag you can put on it...

There are many dancers, many artists, who accept the second best and go along with a fulfillment of themselves that does not entirely satisfy them but seems to be the best they can manage. Nureyev has never been that kind of artist. He has always demanded from himself the highest standards, both technical and artistic. And Nureyev has the idea that he can only keep himself in, not just technical shape, but much more, in artistic shape, by dancing virtually every day. This has been a belief of Nureyev's for years, and oddly enough—for him—it seems to have worked.

People often ask why Nureyev dances every night of his life, if he can. The answer is much more simple than most people imagine. He honestly believes—rightly or wrongly, and on the record, I would say rightly—that his own prowess and abilities are best maintained by this insane work schedule. Some people work in a way that other people do not understand. Nureyev has to be on stage. He is not the kind of dancer who can work in the studio, work and work again in the studio, and still go back to the studio and work even more. This is not the pattern of his personality. Nureyev is enormously dependent on what Tennessee Williams once called "the kindness of strangers." He is enormously dependent upon applause. As a dancer he is only half of himself in the studio. He becomes his full self on the stage. It is not a question of vanity; it is quite simply a question of expressing himself as an artist.

Many dancers have found that they can do things on stage that they never imagined they could do in the studio. With Nureyev this is not merely a matter of accommodation, it is not a matter of trying to excel for the plaudits of the crowd. He needs the very pressure of the theatrical moment. What is in that incandescent moment of reaction between audience and dancer, or if you like of audience and actor? With Nureyev the concept of dancer and actor are absolutely one and the same. He is man poised before an audience. What he is offering is the image of a personality, the concept of a role.

Such a concept of dancing, such a need for performance, such a realization of his role in the theater was totally out of keeping with George Balanchine's perfectly legitimate view of the dancer as an instrument of the choreographer, of the dancer as a servant of the company. They both realized, recognized, and respected this very different viewpoint.

Yet with his enormous lexicon of choreographic knowledge, Nureyev did finally make a late collaboration of sorts with Balanchine. He had already performed in ballets by Balanchine's colleague and fellow artistic director, Jerome Robbins—*Dances at a Gathering*, most notably, which Robbins actually mounted on Nureyev and Anthony Dowell when the Royal Ballet danced it.

In George Balanchine's *Apollo.* Right, photograph by R. Faligant. Left, photograph by Agence de Presse Bernand.

In George Balanchine's *Prodigal Son,* Royal Ballet, 1973. Photograph by Rosemary Winckley.

In 1979, through the intervention of Gert von Gontard, who was co-producing the venture with the New York City Opera, Nureyev performed in a ballet version of Richard Strauss's incidental music to Molière's comedy *Le Bourgeois Gentilhomme*.

Nureyev's old ambition had been fulfilled. Even then it was not easy. Balanchine planned the ballet, started rehearsals, then was taken sick, and Robbins continued, working on Balanchine's original intentions. Finally, Balanchine, restored to health, returned and gave the entire ballet his imprimatur. The last rehearsals were all his, as is almost all of the choreography.

The ballet is one that has always interested Balanchine. In 1932 he made his first version with Tamara Toumanova and David Lichine for René Blum's company in Monte Carlo, with a scenario by Boris Kochno. In 1944 he staged a new version for Serge Denham's Ballets Russes in the United States. For Nureyev and the New York City Opera, he went up to bat for the third time. Kochno's libretto, which has remained unchanged, is a neat abbreviation of the Molière play.

Le Bourgeois Gentilhomme was first presented by the New York City Opera on April 8, 1979, with Patricia McBride, Jean-Pierre Bonnefous, and a corps drawn from the School of American Ballet, joining Nureyev. It has since entered the repertory of Balanchine's New York City Ballet Company, with other casts.

Nureyev's adventures in new choreography have taken several different patterns. He was interested in various European choreographers who were not actually modern-dance choreographers, but who were in some midstream of choreography. Choreographers as diverse as Roland Petit, Maurice Béjart, Rudi van Dantzig, and Hans van Manen were able to offer Nureyev the semblance of modernism, perhaps without the discipline or technique.

As Cleonte in *Le Bourgeois Gentilhomme.* Photograph by Lois Greenfield.

With Patricia McBride and George Balanchine during the mounting of *Le Bourgeois Gentilhomme* on Nureyev and McBride for the New York City Opera, 1979. Photograph by Lois Greenfield.

One of the first of these was Robert Helpmann, who revived his phantasmagoric, Freudian version of *Hamlet* on April 2, 1964, as part of the Shakespeare Anniversary celebration. Elsewhere I have said that Nureyev was born to play Hamlet. He brooded with a glowing intensity, hollow-cheeked, wild of eye and lank of hair, the very image of a prince of most melancholy majesty. It was a role with comparatively little dancing to it, yet, as ever, Nureyev's magnetism and stage projection were formidable, and rarely more so than in this dream-like excursion into the mind and thoughts of the dying Hamlet.

142   In Robert Helpmann's *Hamlet*, set design by Leslie Hurry. Right, with Leslie Edwards in *Hamlet*, Royal Ballet, 1963. Photographs by Reg Wilson.

A critical period in Nureyev's artistic life was when he was moving away from his partnership with Fonteyn, a partnership which had obviously been so important to both of them, so important, in fact, in the history of ballet. The age difference, for one thing, meant that the partnership could not continue indefinitely. Also their aims were different. Although they always admired one another, and still do, they were oddly different dancers. Fonteyn had been totally fulfilled as an artist by her collaboration with Ashton. This was probably the most important aspect of her creative career. Nureyev has never known the close collaboration with any choreographer. He always envied that. In any event, Fonteyn was not prepared at that time to go on the experimental journey that Nureyev so much needed for his fulfillment. The break-up of their partnership was inevitable from that point.

Of course Fonteyn did collaborate in some of Nureyev's experiments with this new world of dance. But the collaborators that she brought in were more inclined to be her older friends, such as Roland Petit, who did indeed provide some modern works for them, but hardly what Nureyev was searching for. Certainly they did their reputations no harm with *Paradise Lost*, for what slender merits the Petit piece had are those of a vehicle, and the two stars rode it triumphantly. Nureyev's fantastic body control, his magnetism, and his animal sense of kinetic value rarely, if ever, looked more sensational.

He has worked with Glen Tetley in several works. He wanted *Pierrot Lunaire*; and he worked very hard to get it. He has worked a great deal with Maurice Béjart whose duet to Mahler's *Songs of a Wayfarer*, created for Nureyev and Bortoluzzi in Brussels in 1971, compared and contrasted two great male dancers. In it Nureyev is seen as something like the questing spirit of man whereas Bortoluzzi is the quieter, more watchful, inner self. The choreography, which is some of the finest that Béjart has ever produced, uses the contemplative Mahler music with considerable subtlety, and manages not only to capture the choreographic style of both men (with Nureyev's prowling heroism and Bortoluzzi's delicate, almost finicky yet strongly defined masculinity) but also something of their characters. It is a very demanding ballet, particularly on Nureyev.

All this he does when it would be so easy for him to rest on his laurels—it would be easier for him in every way, but all the time he tries to extend himself as an artist, to try to become not just older but greater. Like a religious zeal, his motivation is a great love of novelty, a curiosity for the art of dance, a desire not to be out of date. I notice that he always espouses the new; I think it's partly the Diaghilev cry to Jean Cocteau: "Etonnes-moi, Jean." People compare Nureyev—and rightly so—with Nijinsky. I think in some peculiar way he might also be compared with Diaghilev.

With Ghislaine Thesmar in Jerome Robbins' *Afternoon of a Faun*, Paris. Photograph by Colette Masson.

In Maurice Béjart's *Le Sacre du Printemps*, Brussels, 1971. Photograph by Mali/Gamma.

With Paolo Bortoluzzi in Maurice Béjart's *Songs of a Wayfarer*, choreographed on Bortoluzzi and Nureyev in Brussels, 1971. Photograph by Mali/Gamma.

Nureyev's experiments with modern-dance inevitably, eventually, led him to America. In Europe he could work with great talents such as Rudi van Dantzig, Hans van Manen, Kenneth MacMillan. But if he wanted to get to the root of modern-dance, if he wanted to offer himself the alternative to his training, the wary rejection of his classical upbringing, he had to go to the root; he had to come home to America.

Interestingly, Martha Graham was not his first encounter—nor for that matter, his first venture—into modern-dance. He was first attracted to the dance of Paul Taylor. Paul was young, a contemporary of Erik Bruhn, and he presented a type of theatrical dance to which Nureyev could easily relate. Most dancers never go to watch dance performances—they go on state occasions—but Nureyev is a compulsive dance watcher. He is always at dance, and he became very interested in Paul Taylor, very interested in modern-dance generally. When a choreographer interests him, he is prepared to work with him for virtually nothing. Nureyev is often thought of as some kind of avaricious careerist, but in fact he contributes; he will do an enormous amount of performances virtually without fee if a project interests him or out of loyalty. This is true of choreographers, this is true of dancers, this is true of companies. There is no doubt about it; he has been extremely helpful to a number of companies.

I suspect that the first time Nureyev saw Taylor's company was when he and Taylor were in Spoleto in 1964. Nureyev was mounting his production of *Raymonda* for the Royal Ballet in Spoleto, and Taylor was there making his debut. I saw them both. It was very tense. Margot Fonteyn had just been told that her husband, Tito Arias, who had been shot in Panama, had suffered a relapse, and consequently she had to leave. Nureyev had to re-rehearse the entire ballet. It was the first major production he had done in the West—it was his first full-length production. For Taylor it was also a moment of considerable tension. He was making his first trip to Europe, at the same time as the Merce Cunningham troupe, and people were taking sides in that quite customary European political, artistic fashion; so he was very nervous. I remember coming across the two of them having coffee—tea for Rudolf?—in the Spoleto main street, and I was surprised to see them together. I went up to them and said "I did not know you two knew one another." Both of them laughed and said "Why not?" And, of course, why not indeed. They had a lot in common. They had about the same drive. And they also had the same concepts of excellence, the same unbending precision towards themselves and their audiences.

It was soon after that that Nureyev became interested in modern-dance, and eventually he danced with the Taylor Company. I am never sure whether he asked Taylor or Taylor asked him. And I honestly do not believe that either of them could give me the true answer.

In Glen Tetley's *Pierrot Lunaire* for ''Nureyev and Friends'' in New York, 1978.   149
Photograph by Beverley Gallegos.

In Paul Taylor's *Aureole*, Paris, 1971. Photograph by R. Faligant.

It became a matter of conviction between the two of them that Nureyev should dance with the Taylor troupe. He was extremely interested in Taylor's *Aureole*. And Taylor, although at first wondering whether this classically trained animal could indeed find his way through the very difficult passages of modern-dance, decided that when faced with genius, give genius the right of way.

I wonder whether Nureyev knew exactly what he was getting into at this period. I think he may have had the concept that modern-dance was where the men did not wear shoes and the girls did not go up on pointe; but through Taylor he very soon became aware that there was a quite different technique involved. He became very humble about the acquisition of this technique.

The idea of my life in dance is to absorb as much as possible. Paul Taylor, at that time, was not going to cast me in a pathetic Aureole. . . *I had to slave for ten years being trained by Paul. . . I had to prove my good will, my good intentions, that I wanted, that I really was serious, that I do, that I want, for ten years. . . That I do not want to be just star. . .*

Somehow for Nureyev, a prince of the classic ballet, to appear with an American modern-dance company in New York seems just a little as if the Queen of England had confessed to the odd republican sentiment. I am joking, of course. But what Nureyev's appearances with Taylor in *Aureole* showed were his willingness to try anything, his constant eagerness to explore in dance, and, significantly, how the barriers between classic ballet and American modern-dance have now virtually merged.

What Nureyev was really doing here was a favor for Taylor, a gesture of friendship. Nureyev, who performed without fee, arrived from Paris on Sunday, October 13, 1974, rehearsed instantly, gave matinee and evening performances on Monday, and returned to Paris that same night on the ten o'clock plane. He had to dance in Paris the next day. In fact, the money Nureyev brought to the box-office with his two appearances underwrote, in effect, Taylor's entire Broadway season.

Everything gathered together: Nureyev miraculously became part and parcel of Taylor's company. He relaxed into the choreography and danced with precisely Taylor's own gentle, spring-like radiance. Nureyev's simple stage presence carries most things before him like a bulldozer with glitter-dust.

One of his most interesting and most challenging liaisons has been with Martha Graham. She was a giant in her own time with whom Nureyev wanted to work. It was not an easy collaboration. How could it be?

152   In Glen Tetley's *Field Figures*, Royal Ballet, 1971. Photograph by Leslie E. Spatt.

Tristan, choreographed by Glen Tetley on Carolyn Carlson and Nureyev in Paris, 1974.
Photograph by Colette Masson.

It was a surprising combination, which says something not only about Graham and Nureyev, but also about the state of the world of dance. It was both unthinkable and marvelous, this unexpected conjunction of Russia's leading dancer and dance's leading prophetess.

On Nureyev's part is was an act of pure humility. This attitude helped him when he finally went to the Martha Graham school—he was not going as Prince Siegfried, he was going to Martha Graham as a student.

He came from a tradition that would normally have looked down on Martha Graham and everything Martha Graham stood for. You have only to look at that terribly sad and unfortunately so well-documented exchange between Michel Fokine and Martha Graham in the thirties where these two great geniuses of our present dance world came to—not to blows but to such vital misunderstandings that you wonder how they could have talked the same language in the same room. It would have been easy for Nureyev to have taken precisely the view that Fokine had taken, that the ballets, those the classic ballet reveres, were the entire beginning and end of dance. But his curiosity triumphed over everything, and he became bewitched by Martha Graham and everything she stood for.

I was enormously impressed when he went into the Graham repertory. Here he was almost creating a new dance structure for himself; it was something quite different, quite different from any of his earlier achievements. It meant a great deal of sacrifice in terms of work to rehearse with Graham—to try, try all the time to acquire this technique so different from the one he was provided with at the Kirov. He worked at it with an assiduousness, a care and devotion, and perhaps most of all, a sort of driven frenzy that was incredibly impressive.

The question is—what was a dancer like Nureyev doing in a company like that? The brief answer is that he was being passionate. He was certainly not your typical Graham dancer; at times a certain lightness of outline emerged, that special classic grace that no dutifully studied regimen of the contractions and releases basic to the Graham technique could ever obliterate. But in his manner he had a fierceness of belief that was probably closer to the old Martha than anyone else on stage. In the roles he was dancing he was almost unexpectedly effective.

Graham created two roles for him, *Lucifer* and *The Scarlet Letter*, not the ones I especially remember him for in the Graham repertory. In *Night Journey*, when he fell from his bed of shame into the arms of the Chorus, his frozen, silent scream of terror—like Helene Weigel's famous moment in Brecht's *Mother Courage*—seemed to sum up the tragedy. And his sheer presence in *Appalachian Spring*, brooding, moody, and arrogant was unforgettable. To me this was Nureyev absolutely at his height; it showed his power of movement.

In Martha Graham's *Appalachian Spring*, New York, 1975. Photograph by Louis Péres.

Nureyev was the penitent in *El Penitente*. His anguish and eventual joy were most vividly portrayed—his acting and dancing had a wholeheartedness that the new generation of Graham dancers occasionally, in their technical suavity, miss.

He also managed the duality of the character in *Lucifer* with exceptional subtlety. He danced the choreography with a natural authority that was all the more remarkable in that, unannounced, he was dancing throughout the evening with an injured ankle. At that Gala performance where ticket prices ranged from fifty to ten thousand dollars, Martha Graham, with a little help from her friends, raised about two hundred thousand dollars in a single performance, breaking every Broadway house record known to man.

It was not merely with Martha Graham that Nureyev was content. He knew other forms and other styles of modern-dance. And this attracted him to the Dance Company of Murray Louis. Murray Louis comes from a quite different dance tradition than that of Martha Graham. Most of American modern-dance can be directly related to the Denishawn School, founded by Ruth St. Denis and Ted Shawn, in the twenties. This school developed Martha Graham and Doris Humphrey, who later became the two founding mothers, in effect, of American modern-dance. Their techniques were slightly dissimilar and their styles were radically different, but their aims were remarkably the same.

In the thirties there came into American modern-dance another factor. This was the influence of German modern-dance, which came from Mary Wigman. Wigman, herself, never worked extensively in the United States, although she did appear here. But her disciple, Hanya Holm, was a prominent and significant figure in the American modern-dance field. She gave birth—if that is the expression—to a whole school of American modern-dance, of whom the most important proponents were Alwin Nikolais and Murray Louis.

This was another new kind of dance for Nureyev, different from his classical school, different from the Grahamesque schooling that he had been accustomed to in modern-dance. It was vibrant, abrupt, based very much on rhythmic gesture, having a febrile intensity that he had not previously encountered. He became fascinated with Louis and his dancing, and was soon asking Louis to do work for him. And thus began another very vital collaboration of Nureyev and the American modern-dance.

As an artist Nureyev has clearly been through many periods. One can trace his Kirov beginnings, his Pushkin period, his desire to be the ultimate romantic classical dancer. Then one sees his adventures in European modern-dance, and then his further adventures with American modern-dance. Interestingly, they each stand up as an entire artistic experience. He's never given anything up when he took something else for himself. He has used all these experiences to enlarge his range.

In Martha Graham's *El Penitente*, New York, 1977. Photograph by Beverley Gallegos.

158   In *Lucifer*, choreographed on Nureyev by Martha Graham in 1975.

In *The Scarlet Letter*, choreographed on Nureyev by Martha Graham in 1977.
Photographs by Beverley Gallegos.

Also, he has been extraordinarily adept at finding roles that suited him for each particular period in his life. Sometimes these had been roles that had been created for him. Sometimes they had been roles that he had noticed and realized that he could dance, and that they would be suitable for him. He has used his career with extraordinary sensitivity, and, even more, sensibility. He always gives the impression of a man who knows exactly what he is doing at any moment. He is careful of his career. He is careful of his art. And he knows exactly how to put the pressure points on his career so that they will have their full effectiveness.

The interesting thing is that this approach to his art has no element of personal vanity about it. He is the least vain man that you are going to meet. He is a man who merely is driven by some platonic ideal of dance and wishes to fulfill that ideal in any way he can. He uses choreographers as collaborators. Oddly enough he uses them as if they were doing something for him, rather than he doing something for them. This is a very serious relationship between the performing artist and the creative artist. It is a relationship that most creative artists find difficult to sustain. And it was probably no accident that Balanchine, without mentioning this aspect of their proposed collaboration, would have found peculiarly difficult to handle. Nureyev always feels that he needs the input of a choreographer, also that he needs to contribute himself.

Like the other great Russian émigrés of recent years, Nureyev has taken to the best in Western choreography. Here you can watch a dancer stepping through a range of contemporary choreography and giving everything his own imprint.

Periodically Nureyev is in New York presenting his *Nureyev and Friends* programs to sold-out houses on Broadway. The idea is gloriously extravagant. For example, in 1974 there were thirty-four performances and Nureyev danced not only at every performance, but in every ballet at every performance. Anna Pavlova pushed herself hard, but never like this. Nureyev, who faced this massive stint with smiling composure, was perfectly confident.

In the 1975 program, Nureyev danced five times at each performance. Even in terms of endurance this is fantastic, and in terms of versatility of style and technique, this brilliant program could well serve as Mr. Nureyev's calling card to the world.

The variety and balance of roles offered in these almost-yearly programs provides new audiences with programs that go far in exploring the entire range of dance as well as showing the artistry, virtuosity, versatility and inquiring spirit of Nureyev. There has never been a dancer quite so dedicated to his art.

It is rather simple to be a genius. You just have to be born with genius, be careful, and get lucky. But to be a genius who is also a legend is something quite different. A genius can exist in a vacuum; a legend turns the world around him. Rudolf Nureyev is going down in history as one of those emblematic dance names—a Vestris or a Nijinsky, or in more popular terms, a Pavlova, perhaps. I have seen men with more technique, and I have seen men with more perfection of style, more harmony of classic gesture. But I have never seen any dancer—not even my adored Fonteyn, or even Martha Graham—whose movements have so burned themselves on my mind like a brand. I shall recall Nureyev in a series of unforgettable photographs that only my memory took and my heart filtered.

He is one of those terribly few artists whom it is a privilege to see. He dances with his mind and his heart.

One of the things that has made Nureyev legendary is his energy. He goes on and on and gives performance after performance—and these performances are remarkably consistent. Yes, he does have off nights—everyone does—but very rarely. This consistency is what I notice to be an extraordinary part of Nureyev's action. He could even be dancing with a broken leg, but the outline, the special image of his performance will not vary a jot. His dramatic image—his power of impinging on memory—is unsurpassable.

Nureyev, Olivier. They both have the same kind of theatrical talents. The same ability to remain the same and yet to do something completely different, the same physical skills, and the same abandonment in the steambath of a theater. I discover that watching Olivier was a great apprenticeship for watching Nureyev.

Another thing that has made Nureyev a legend is his availability. He has been seen everywhere. During the past two decades, Nureyev has been flamboyantly and magically visible. He is a pop star in a way that no other dancer has ever been. He is as associated with dance in the public mind as Valentino was associated with the silent movie.

Fame had been difficult for him to handle—so far as critics are concerned, he reads everyone and is disconcerted by anything less than a jet-propelled rave. Yet this questing aspect of his career is obviously what makes Rudolf run and jump, and bleed—a little.

Nureyev never stops. He is a man dedicated to survival, perfection, and self-improvement; he also resents physical injury. Illnesses and injuries that would have most other dancers on crutches or in bed, he shakes off with a mixture of willpower, bandages, and pain-killers. He goes on and on.

I once thought that Rudolf the wild was the enemy of Nureyev the artist; I am coming to accept that his effectiveness is a product of the tensions between the two, with that element of unstylishness in his dancing making his stylishness individual.

Everything is subjugated to his flamboyant temperament, while his temperament is not subjugated to anything. Even his curtain calls are miniature and, I imagine, quite instinctive performances in themselves. Just to see him glare furiously at a conductor is to be made forcibly aware of a presence that is remarkably un-British. The red velvet curtains part discreetly, and the star—lean and hungry look complete—reaches his Covent Garden public. The performance is over, but the performance has actually only begun. In these carefully choreographed calls, the instinctive arrogance blended with natural charm, the little-boy-lost merging with the Tatar chief, in this moment of communication between himself and his audience, Nureyev satisfyingly becomes his own legend.

He stands there like a matador—if only a ballet had ears he would be given them by his adoring public. He has not merely danced a ballet, he seems to have fulfilled some psychic need of his audience, and this is the moment they all share. Rudolf Nureyev—in dance at least—is Public Idol Number One. And his charms, his charisma, go beyond the dance world. For many people who have no real interest in ballet, Nureyev is a symbol of the dance, a recognizable and acceptable link between themselves and an art they would normally have disregarded.

The force of Nureyev's personality grows stronger and stronger, and he has a wonderful eloquence in his dance phrasing. We need a comparable word in dance for what in music is called tone. It is something apart from technique, and certainly apart from characterization. It has a great deal to do with individuality. Nureyev's dancing has the most wonderful tone to it. Note also the way he varies his entire way of dancing to serve the choreography. The gently stern Nureyev of *Apollo* is quite different from the playful but immaculate classicist of Bournonville. Yet in everything he does—as with every great artist—a residual persona persists.

No other individual dancer has been able to achieve anything similar except Isadora Duncan, Anna Pavlova, and Martha Graham. Undoubtedly Vaslav Nijinsky and Margot Fonteyn could have, but never tried.

If one person could be called the world's greatest dancer, it would just have to be Rudolf Nureyev. The quality of greatness in a dancer is as indefinable as beauty. One can draw up a list of virtues a great dancer would be expected to possess, and when a neat line has been drawn under the total you would have missed the one essential thing that transforms the merely magnificent into the truly great. In the final analysis you are brought back to the idea that a great dancer is a dancer whom a sufficient number of people, all sufficiently well-informed, think great. Most audiences clearly think that in Rudolf Nureyev they are seeing a great dancer; I believe those judgments will be confirmed in time by the knowledgeable ballet public. Make no mistake, he is the sort of dancer on whom legends alight.

Curtain call after a performance of *Le Corsaire*. Photograph by Leslie E. Spatt.

THE CATALYST

Maurice Béjart has defined the twentieth century as the century of dance. Whether or not this is true remains to be seen. One thing that is certain, however, is that dance in the twentieth century has won wider popularity and, even more significant, wider acceptance as a major art form, than was so in the years before the present era, when dancing and particularly ballet were regarded as little more than light forms of entertainment.

The figures who have influenced twentieth century ballet may be grouped under two major headings. There were those who might be called innovators, and those who might be called popularizers. In each category there were many people, and some of them obviously more important than others. Perhaps the four most significant figures in the early part of this century—and they made a strangely diverse quartet—were Serge Diaghilev, the impresario, Vaslav Nijinsky, his principal male dancer and source of inspiration, Anna Pavlova, and Isadora Duncan. To some extent, these are symbolic figures. For example, it could be cogently argued that Michel Fokine, with his five principles and his reassertion of the doctrine of Jean Georges Noverre, with its new emphasis on ballet as communication rather than as decoration, played a more vital artistic role than any single one of the quartet mentioned above. Yet it was those four who somehow penetrated the psyche and the consciousness of early twentieth century imagination. What did they do?

Let us first take Diaghilev and his protegé Nijinsky. Diaghilev was a pragmatic entrepreneur. He encountered ballet as an after-dinner entertainment and transformed it into an after-dinner art form. He found it glittering and left it chic. He also recognized the strength of ballet tradition in his homeland, Russia, and particularly in his adopted hometown, St. Petersburg. Finally he also saw ballet's potentialities as a major art form in the century ahead.

Diaghilev relied extensively on the theories and, for that matter, the practice of Fokine. The creative element in the Diaghilev company was to a very large extent provided by Alexandre Benois and Michel Fokine, as well as the other artists surrounding them, such as Leon Bakst—like Benois a designer—and the composer Igor Stravinsky. If it was Fokine's

In his production of *Raymonda*, Act 3 for the Australian Ballet. Photograph by Dina Makarova.

concept to make dance expressive from head to toe, it was Diaghilev who realized that dance had to be made an expression of man, and ballet an ideal blend of the arts, one in which dance, music, and design play equal parts in the fulfillment of significant dramatic expression. This was Diaghilev's unique and particular innovation—even if he had adopted it from the theory of a director of the Imperial theaters. Vsevolojsky, the creative mind behind the 1898 production of *The Sleeping Beauty* in St. Petersburg, who here contrived the first modern ballet, to the degree that it offered a combination of all the theatrical arts. Diaghilev saw, too, that audiences were tired of full evening spectacles, which was convenient for him economically. He sensed as well the readiness of Paris for an introduction to the surge of Russian culture which characterized the years immediately before the Revolution of 1917.

The history of the Diaghilev ballet from its first appearance in Paris in 1906 to its final dissolution with Diaghilev's death in 1929, is one of the most fascinating chronicles of ballet history. Never before or since, has there been a company so much infused with the character and mettle of one individual. To a large extent, the Diaghilev ballet was an extension of Diaghilev's taste. In no absolute way creative, he was yet the cause of creation in others. In short, he was a catalyst. His abilities were largely pragmatic and he made the best of what he had. When he had dancers, he used dancers. When he had no dancers, he used choreographers. When he had no choreographers, he used designers. Such was almost the history of his company. He was able to make ballet original and daring, when it needed most to be just that. Yet he never lost sight of his classical roots—witness his experiment, perhaps his most audacious experiment of all, with the 1921 London revival of *The Sleeping Princess.* It must be remembered that not only was his company the extension of his own taste, it was practically the extension of his own salon. The Diaghilev Ballet was distinctly a company for the rich and the cultivated. It was what would nowadays be termed, somewhat disparagingly, determinedly elitist.

Isadora Duncan, the other major innovator in the early years of the twentieth century dance could hardly be more dissimilar to the artistocratic Diaghilev. Unlike Diaghilev, Isadora was a creator in her own right. Unlike him again she was completely uncompromising in her dealings with society. She never formed a company or left a tradition, and her influence on the dance world of her time was very much peripheral. She was not part of any dance tradition; indeed her very innovation implied a break with dance tradition. Her achievement was to demonstrate that Americans could dance. As she shared with her countrymen very little formal classic training, she found herself dancing in her own way and in her own style. Her innovations were enormous in the force of their rupture with hitherto hallowed classic traditions. She also chose to explore a different type of subject matter in dance, more heroic, grander, more passionate. She also started to dance to great music.

A pause in rehearsal. Milan, 1980. Photograph by Fornaciari/Gamma.

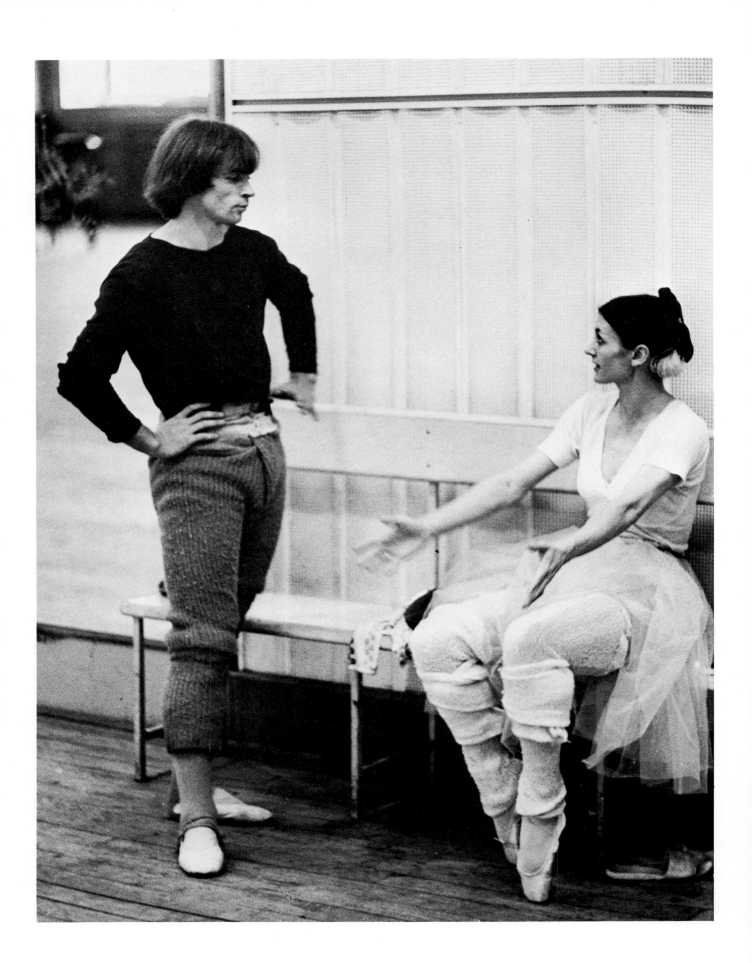

While Petipa was using a Minkus for the most part, a Glazounov when he was lucky, or, when he was very lucky, a Tchaikovsky, Isadora Duncan deliberately chose Beethoven. All this had a profound effect on classic ballet—particularly on Fokine. Duncan and her theories of free style in dance as the untrammeled expression of soul found some echo in the Diaghilev ballet.

However it was in other areas of dance that Duncan's influence was most felt—not so much her influence, perhaps, as her inspiration. With her insistence on the possibility of dance expressionism, Duncan provided the impetus to the entire expressive dance movement, laying the foundation for the modern movement in American dance, with all the international ramifications it has given birth to.

These then were two of the innovators. There were to be many others. Nijinsky and Pavlova were somewhat different. They were not innovators in any real sense; they were popularizers. Nijinsky had a curious historic part to play in the development of modern ballet. Had Diaghilev not fallen in love with him, it is entirely conceivable that Diaghilev would not have been inspired to create the Ballets Russes in the first place and to take it to Paris in the second. Until he met Nijinsky, Diaghilev's interests were very much concentrated on painting and on opera rather than on ballet. The liaison with Nijinsky seemed to provide the necessary grit to make the pearl.

Nijinsky's crucial importance goes beyond that mere historic accident. Nijinsky was the first male dancer to reestablish the equality of the male since the days of Perrot, or, some would say, Vestris. During the latter third of the nineteenth century, the male dancer, who had at the beginning of ballet's history been the paramount partner, fell into low repute. He was merely a porteur, an appendage to the ballerina, intended to make the ballerina look light, graceful, and weightless, and to provide some credence to the story line. Very often, particularly outside Russia and Denmark, he did not even get the opportunity to dance, and in some places, particularly France, he was removed altogether. Many ballets, such as the first performance of *Coppélia* in 1870, were performed with the male part danced *en travesti* by a woman. The sheer genius of Nijinsky, both as a dancer, and very clearly as a personality, changed all that, brought a new popularity to male dancing, and a new understanding of the male in ballet.

If Nijinsky did something for the popularity of the male in ballet, that was nothing to the popularity that Anna Pavlova brought to the art of ballet as a whole. Pavlova was one of that incredible generation of Maryinsky ballerinas between the years of 1890 and 1910 who were to exert a considerable influence on the history of dance, both by the impeccable standards of their performances, and later, in many instances, with the new qualities of their teaching.

It was Pavlova who went outside the court and social circles favored by Diaghilev, and went to the people. From the middle days of her career until her death in 1931, Pavlova became a tireless proselytizer for dance. For all the people who saw the Diaghilev ballet, many more people all over the world saw Pavlova in her countless tours. It was Pavlova, rather than Diaghilev, who inspired a whole generation of new dancers. Certainly Diaghilev gave many opportunities to major choreographers, but it was Pavlova who provided the first impression of a ballerina dancing, it was Pavlova who caused dancers—men as well as women—to go to dancing school. She was in that way one of the major catalysts of twentieth century ballet.

After these four, the history of twentieth century ballet is strewn with innovators and popularizers. One popularizer, nowadays little recognized, was Colonel Vassily de Basil, an entrepreneur quite different from Diaghilev. He was the creator of the Ballet Russe de Monte Carlo, which underwent many changes of name, direction, and fortunes over the next two decades. In 1933, he brought a new wave of ballet popularity to the world, particularly to the English-speaking world. In a sense he combined the mass popularity of Anna Pavlova with the more elaborate spectacles of Serge Diaghilev and helped to lay the foundation for the art of classic ballet as we now know it throughout the world.

There were of course many others: the innovator Lincoln Kirstein, the popularizer Lucia Chase, the innovators Ninette de Valois and Marie Rambert, choreographers Frederick Ashton, George Balanchine, and Antony Tudor, and certain dancers who brought the art of dance to larger and larger audiences. Notable among these was probably, the modern Pavlova, Margot Fonteyn, who enjoyed a longer career than any classic dancer before her. Then there were the innovators in modern-dance—Ruth St. Denis, Ted Shawn, and their artistic progeny Martha Graham and Doris Humphrey. The ferment of dance after World War II paid a peculiar testimony to most of these people, many of whom had really only started their life work.

After World War II it became evident that world dance was changing in a very remarkable fashion. At one time there had been nothing but national dance. There had been French dance, there had been Italian dance, there had been Russian dance, and although there had never been anything specifically either English or American about classic dance, Britain, the United States and other countries provided a haven for visiting companies. After the general decadence of ballet at the end of the nineteenth century, when all its early promise in the romantic era had died away, and ballet had been reduced to vapidity in every country with the exceptions of Denmark and Russia, the revival of ballet interest at the beginning of the present century was essentially an international movement. It started obviously with the expatriate Russians, but very soon the Diaghilev ballet and the continuations of that company

With Roland Petit during the mounting of *Paradise Lost* on Fonteyn and Nureyev for the Royal Ballet, 1964. Photograph by Giancarlo Botti/Monique Valentin.

171

demonstrated a far more international profile. The specifically Russian element was modified by a large dose of Parisian taste. England and America eventually exerted their influence on the expatriate Ballets Russes, and, as after the Revolution, the sources of Russian dance dried up, many dancers of other nationalities were recruited into the so-called Ballets Russes. But the Ballet Russe as an international touring concept was doomed, effectively destroyed during World War II.

During and after the war, national ballets emerged all over the world, each with its own characteristics, its own national choreographers, its own accents in the common language of dance. In America this language was strongly tinged by the special accent of American modern-dance, a dance discipline that grew up and intertwined with the classic ballet in America. In time, this same modern-dance idiom crossed the Atlantic and settled in Great Britain. So both British and American dance are unusual in combining both elements in their choreographic culture.

The world of dance in these postwar years was a world of interdependence and mutual influence. There was a great deal of touring: American companies went to Britain, British companies came to America, the Paris Opéra toured widely, Dutch companies started to tour, companies developed in Germany. There was considerable cultural interplay.

The one place where this interchange of dance ideas had no currency was in Soviet Russia. It was here that ballet had been frozen since the 1917 Revolution. That is perhaps not quite fair. Immediately following the Revolution, there was a considerable degree of radical dance experimentation—experimentation indeed in all branches of the theater. It was a great period—the time of Stanislavsky and Meyerhold, of the great constructivists Pevsner and Nabor. There were interesting and productive years in Soviet Art, when the first strains of revolutionary freedom made themselves felt in the bloodstream of the country's culture.

But very soon, during the twenties, through the iron-clad concept of Socialist Realism, which demanded that every artistic act revealed a social purpose, Soviet art tended to become ossified. Curiously enough, this mattered much less in ballet than in any of the other art forms. This was largely because in ballet, Socialist Realism fitted quite well into the creative development of Russian dance as it had been initiated by Fokine. Fokine himself, if you study his five principles of choreography, would probably have had little difficulty in relating to Socialist Realism. And indeed the greatest triumph of Socialist Realism in Soviet ballet, Lavrovsky's *Romeo and Juliet,* could well be seen as the high point of Fokinian ballet making. Yet it was a stultifying place for a young man to grow up in. And the Kirov Ballet offered very few insights into the international dance world.

Photograph by Giancarlo Botti/Liaison Agency.

There have been other significant, even great, male dancers in the twentieth century. There were positively cohorts and regiments of superb male dancers. They ranged from Leonide Massine to Stanislav Idzikovsky, from Anton Dolin to Serge Lifar, and a little later, from André Eglevsky to Igor Youskevitch. But none of them really impinged on the popular consciousness.

When Nureyev came to the West in 1961 he had very little concrete knowledge of the world he was entering. Certainly he had seized whatever opportunities his native Russia had permitted to glimpse something of the diversity of Western dance, but such exposure had been inevitably brief, tantalizing, and inconclusive. He subscribed to certain myths about Western ballet, entertained certain fantasies—perhaps extravagant ones—about it. In a young man's dream he saw himself studying with particular Western teachers, performing the works of celebrated Western choreographers, dancing with Western companies of international renown. And all of this flowed from an urgent desire and will to extend himself artistically, to experience what was new, to enter a realm of personal, professional, and emotional freedom.

Nureyev was a strange Eastern growth, and he flourished in this new Western soil. Almost from the very beginning, it was evident that the alliance of Western soil and Eastern growth would bring into being a new phenomenon of generous mutual enrichment. Within the decade, Nureyev began to emerge as a major catalyst in the procession of twentieth-century ballet—indeed, twentieth-century dance in almost all its manifestations. What was singular about the nature of the role that one saw an inescapable part of Nureyev's destiny, was its unique blend of the force of the innovator with the influence of the popularizer. Diaghilev and Pavlova: for the first time in the history of dance, the individual powers of their separate spheres merged, and the burden as well as the splendor of that fusion was to rest upon the capacity and visionary enterprise of Rudolf Nureyev.

The impact of this change in dance fortunes may be assessed from many points of vantage. There was, first of all, the value—as sheer sensation—of Nureyev's presence. Even his defection, however unintentionally, occasioned notoriety,—initially far in excess of his fame as a dancer—that instantly wrote headlines in the Western world. It invested him with the attributes of an alien phenomenon, the allure of a sacred monster—an exoticism to be watched, studied, analyzed. There can be no doubt that had Nureyev not defected, he would not have attracted the great weight of public notoriety that attended the early years of his career. Of course, not all of this was to his advantage. It distressed him as often as it made possible for him certain opportunities that would not have been available to another dancer erupting on the world in less sensational circumstances. Yet Nureyev did not falter or lose his way under the blaze of scrutiny. He parried and used his notoriety well, taking from it what he wanted or needed and discarding what might have hurt him. For a young man at that time he showed a considerable and uncommon maturity. It was a maturity that would stand him in good stead as he set about examining the options that were to fashion his future career.

Nureyev accepted with alacrity Ninette de Valois' invitation to join the Royal Ballet as a permanent guest artist, and there is a sense in which it is legitimate to say that he was to be the final link in her chain of vision. In the briefest of possible times—approximately thirty years, even less—Ninette de Valois had created what was in effect a great national company, not unworthy of comparison—in stature and dimension—with the Kirov or the Bolshoi companies. She had assembled a major repertory, much of it appropriated from the classic Russian Imperial legacy, but one which also offered a lively range of indigenous modern British works and a few examples selected from other schools and genres of twentieth-century international ballet. She had remarkable dancers, including a whole pleiade of potential ballerinas arranged in constellation around the central radiance of her great ballerina and star, Margot Fonteyn.

Yet de Valois recognized that the one most vulnerable element in British ballet—the one crucially weak link in her chain—was the caliber of male dancing. The company had certainly enjoyed the presence of exceptional male dancers in various phases of its history. Harold Turner, the demi-caractère dancer who created the "Blue Skater" in Frederick Ashton's *Les Patineurs,* was possibly unexcelled as a virtuoso dancer in the West during the thirties and forties. Michael Somes, Fonteyn's partner of long and distinguished standing, was a danseur noble of the greatest elegance and style. David Blair, who was partnering Fonteyn at the time of Nureyev's emergence, was also an artist of outstanding quality, although primarily a demi-caractère dancer. Yet the male dancer in British ballet—the generality—could rarely if ever match his Soviet counterpart in finish, conviction, passion, and even technique. De Valois knew this, and she also recognized at once that in Nureyev she was seeing something more than a standard Soviet male dancer. She knew that she was in the presence of a Promethean torch-bearer of the male in dance, an artist and dancer whom time and history would rank with Nijinsky and Vestris.

Practically, she was aware also that the presence of Nureyev would raise the level of her entire company. She saw it as a historical necessity—an artistic destiny—that Nureyev should join the Royal Ballet. And she had her way. The impact of Rudolf Nureyev on the Royal Ballet was instantaneous and almost convulsive. He aroused more interest in the Royal Ballet than it had ever been able to exert by itself alone. He commanded the allure of a wholly different kind of male dancer, altogether a much more arresting and magnetic figure than the British public and press were accustomed to. He was more athletic, he jumped dazzlingly higher, he was more flamboyant in manner, yet equally more classical in style.

From the very beginning, Nureyev showed himself as willing to teach as he was to learn. He was always open to criticism, even if sometimes, on the surface, that criticism might seem to be contemptuously received. Ashton has said of Nureyev: "He is as true to his schooling as to a religion. If he couldn't dance, he would beg." And John Field, assistant director of the company at that time, tells of a long overseas tour with Nureyev, and how "always he was prepared to work. No detail was too small for him, nothing too unimportant. He is a man totally committed to his job." In class, he was always ready to assist other dancers, always liberal in coaching and encouraging his colleagues—even when his manner of not suffering fools gladly gave that encouragement an occasional unfortunate edge, and his well-intentioned advice was sometimes taken amiss. In this fashion, Nureyev slowly entered upon his absorption into the web of Western ballet in general, and Britain's Royal Ballet in particular.

However, this process of absorption was not to be negotiated without its share of snarls, many of them minor, some of them graver in import. The rapturous popular admiration Nureyev's dancing evoked inevitably provoked envy in some quarters. And his inimitable personal deportment on stage as well as off—the way he stood, his mannerisms, the histrionic fashion in which he took curtain calls, his casual habit of walking in and out of the classroom—much of this tended to be imitated by the younger men in the company. One ballet master rebuked a young member of the corps "who behaved every bit as badly as Nureyev, but unluckily did not dance one-tenth as well." Other male dancers responded to his presence in contradictory and unpredictable ways—the established David Blair was notably discouraged; the rising Anthony Dowell and David Wall found in him a vital source of inspiration and example.

In the world outside, there was an elusive fear that Nureyev was somehow disturbing the decorous tenor of the traditional Royal Ballet style, an apprehension that his cavalier disposition toward established choreographies—particularly those nineteenth century classics to whose conservation British tradition had staunchly and quite properly dedicated itself—might have subversive and even destructive consequences. Finally, there was a fear that in the end Nureyev's effect on Fonteyn would prove deleterious—ultimately, as one would see, the most groundless of all those apprehensions. These sentiments and anxieties were expressed freely in London and even in New York—at that time, quite literally, the Royal Ballet's second home. Indeed, the former critic of the *New York Times*, John Martin, writing in *The Saturday Review* of a Fonteyn-Nureyev performance, observed that it offered the spectacle of a princess dancing with a gigolo. Still, Nureyev persevered.

Rehearsing *Paradise Lost* with Margot Fonteyn. Photograph by Reg Wilson/Camera Press, Ltd.

When Dame Margot first danced *Giselle* with Nureyev, some kind of magic occured, and against all probability and even possibility Dame Margot entered a new career. The factor that distinguished Dame Margot's later career from that of her predecessors is simply, yet totally impossibly, the fact that she had technically improved beyond the age when dancers can improve. The catalyst of Nureyev had created a new dancer of her. The effect that Nureyev had on Fonteyn's career was unbelievable. In fact he more than recycled it—he motorized it.

. . . there was an exchange, and there was incredible contradiction, like technical things. Apparently I did suggest and then sit quiet; at rehearsal with ballerinas, I did suggest this and that; it did work; and suddenly, she could do those thirty-two fouettés! Suddenly she could do all those things. . . There was a lot of contradictions, but at the same time we did work, the good will was there. . .

178   With Margot Fonteyn, Frederick Ashton and John Hart during Nureyev's staging of *Le Corsaire* pas de deux for the Royal Ballet, 1962. Photograph by Reg Wilson/Camera Press Ltd.

He inspired Fonteyn, inspired her to even greater heights at a point in her career when she should, by all the usual laws which govern a career, be descending from them. That in itself is something quite remarkable.

I suspect that during this period it would have taken a rash prophet to predict that Nureyev would someday exert the influence on classic dance that time and the future have ratified. Certainly he was a great dancer, a touchstone, and even a landmark in the history of dance in our time. Clearly he exhibited the makings of a notable coach and perhaps a great teacher. But in the young Russian we saw performing with the Royal Ballet in that first year of freedom in the West, there was little to suggest the lurking possibility and potentiality of one of the major ballet masters and regisseurs in twentieth century dance. The world was to come to that awareness unexpectedly, and rather sooner than one might have imagined.

The question arose of what repertory he and Fonteyn might dance Nureyev suggested to Ninette de Valois that he mount for the Royal Ballet the Kingdom of the Shades scene from *La Bayadère*, which had been performed in London and Paris by the Kirov Ballet in 1961. At that time it had been recognized and acclaimed by connoisseurs as a touchstone of Petipa's choreography, indisputably one of the masterpieces of Russian ballet. Since the Royal Ballet already had the major works of Petipa and Ivanov in its repertory, the choice seemed a desirable one. Yet the decision to entrust it to the still unknown capacities of Nureyev was a bold one.

I remember well the derision provoked—in both the ballet audience and the ballet press—at the announcement that Nureyev would stage the scene from *La Bayadère*. Why, the general sentiment went, should *this* Russian firebird be assumed to possess a special ability to recreate Petipa's choreography? He had not been with the Kirov for long; he had been only a principal dancer; he had not been involved in any of the major artistic decisions of the company; nor had he had any previous experience as régisseur or as ballet master. Nureyev, too, was conscious of what responsibility lay before him. "I feel like a conductor in front of an orchestra," he said at the time of that first production. "It is a great thrill to see dancers respond to you. You take a group of people and then you realize you can do something with them."

The turbulent success of that opening night at Covent Garden on November 27, 1963 abolished all anxiety. From the opening moment, the audience saw the ensemble of the Royal Ballet dancing with a precision and eloquence few could recall in its recent history. Nureyev had reproduced the choreography—still fresh in the memory of London audiences

from the Kirov performances of only two previous seasons—with what seemed a meticulous authority. He particularly informed the solo parts with a signal intensity. Indeed, when he found one of his own solos not working to his personal satisfaction, he rushed off the stage in the middle of it—leaving the startled conductor to go it alone. That sudden flash of temperament did provoke considerable comment in the press the next morning. It also revealed something of Nureyev's sense of aesthetic responsibility.

Most important, Nureyev drew from those English dancers something entirely special to themselves, as well as infusing them with the requisite Russian style. They performed this old Russian classic with the beginning of that exultant manner, uniquely their own, that would become the trademark of the Royal Ballet.

It was this that overwhelmed the British audience and press that night—the presence of a different brand of talent in Nureyev. It was apparent that he was not solely a dancer who was going to flash his brief hour on the stage. What had been triumphantly demonstrated was the possibility of a major new resource for Western ballet.

Confirmed by the impact and success of his production of *La Bayadère*, Nureyev began to look about for new territory to explore. At first, evidence of his touch was to been seen chiefly in rearrangements of solos and certain classical *pas de deux*, (for example the celebrated *Le Corsaire*) for himself and his partners. He interpolated passages into the Royal Ballet's production of *The Sleeping Beauty* (not to universal happiness, it must be admitted), and on occasion, significantly altered the performances of other dancers who followed him in roles on which he had brought to bear his particular angle of vision. For example, when Svetlana Beriosova and Donald MacLeary danced *Giselle* for the first time after Nureyev's debut with Fonteyn in that work, they adopted many of the innovations that he had introduced. In particular, Nureyev's refashioning of the close of the ballet—with Albrecht left in solitary wonderment—bringing the story to a far more poetic and satisfying conclusion than earlier versions. Moreover, the freedom Nureyev took in his acting gave many of the British dancers the cue, or, perhaps more accurately, the precedent, to invest the old mime with a more naturalistic air and sensibility.

What gradually became evident was that the young Russian was marshalling his powers to mount his own productions of the full-length extant Russian classics—the Tchaikovsky masterworks *Swan Lake*, *The Sleeping Beauty*, and *The Nutcracker*—and endow them with the fresh legacy of his Soviet choreographic approach.

Ever since his arrival in the West, Nureyev had chafed at the conventional Western conception of classical production, particularly the view he saw dominating British ballet. The

With Gelsey Kirkland in *Le Corsaire* at the 35th Anniversary Gala of American Ballet Theatre, New York. Photograph by Jack Vartoogian.

problem of choreographic restatement he saw as akin to the problem confronting a contemporary director when he undertook to stage a classic play. Nureyev maintained—cogently, by his own lights—that it was unnatural for contemporary choreographers and dancers, let alone audiences, to insist on a strict adherence to what they took to be the original Petipa or Ivanov choreography. His argument was sustained in a parallel area by the radical transformations in Shakespearean production that Peter Brook and Peter Hall were making in the British theater.

> *. . . but basically start your piece with Petipa. I try to find equivalent of what Petipa would have made impact in 1890; to find equivalent for today in today's terms.*

Here, of course, Nureyev was in the mainstream of Soviet tradition. Soviet ballet has never made a pretense of trying to maintain scrupulously the original choreography of works that are in its domain. A few set images from Ivanov's *Swan Lake*, several unique choreographic excerpts such as the Kingdom of the Shades scene from *La Bayadère*, certain dances such as the Rose Adagio from *The Sleeping Beauty* have been retained and maintained as examples and touchstones of the old style. But for the rest, Soviet ballet masters have felt free to change what they will, including, on occasion, the story. This was the tradition from which Nureyev sprang and which had nurtured him, and he was soon to set about adopting it to the Western repertory.

But he was still a young and unseasoned choreographer, and before he would undertake so intimidating an enterprise, Nureyev chose to try his hand at something more in the manner of reconstruction, akin to what he had accomplished with *La Bayadère*. This was to be his production of the full-length *Raymonda*, mounted for the second company of the Royal Ballet, and given its first performance at the Spoleto Festival in June of 1964.

It should be remembered that *Raymonda*—especially its last act—is one of the few ballets that has remained more or less choreographically intact in the Soviet Union, particularly at the Kirov Ballet. Certainly Nureyev was conscious of this: "I think the main purpose of ballet is dancing," he observed eloquently, "and this is why I revere Petipa." That reverence was reflected in the stylistic tact with which he approached *Raymonda*—much as he had the earlier *La Bayadère*—as well as a new boldness of attack in negotiating the story and the score.

> *Petipa had sweeping diagonals, he moved, the movement on stage was spatial. . .*

The full-length *Raymonda* was almost unknown in the West, although a Lithuanian company had danced it in London in the nineteen thirties, and, a decade later, George Balanchine and Alexandra Danilova had mounted it for the Ballets Russes de Monte Carlo. Nureyev, presumably recognizing that the story—when it is not absurdly complex—is still

182

184   With Marilyn Jones in his production of *Raymonda*, Act 3 for the Australian Ballet, New York, 1970.
Photograph by Dina Makarova.

rather lacking in an essential human interest, attempted at once to make more sense of it than had previously been done, even in Soviet productions. He jettisoned as much of the story as he possibly dared, doing away also with the scenario's realistic castle in France, framing it with gauzes and scenes run up by the designer, Beni Montresor. For this first production for a Western company he chose to give a skeletal version of the work, setting it much as he might one of Balanchine's plotless ballets. He kept as much of the choreography as he could remember, although adding to it many bridge passages of his own—in the Petipa style—and generally tightening up sharply the narrative line of this medieval princess who dreams of her two lovers: one sacred and the other very much profane.

The principal roles had originally been set for Margot Fonteyn and Nureyev himself. Unfortunately, those first performances in Spoleto were thrown into chaos by Fonteyn's husband's relapse after the assassination attempt in Panama, compelling her to fly to his bedside. The premiere fell to her understudy, Doreen Wells, who acquitted herself excellently. By the end of the season, Fonteyn was able to dance one matinee.

As Jean de Brienne, Raymonda's courtly lover, Nureyev danced with a lively contempt for gravity, and with that tigerish, masculine pounce uniquely his. Perhaps of even more ultimate importance, he was able to instill something of that quality, as well as an approximation of the correct Kirov manner, into the male ensemble, offering the dancers opportunities that they seized with vigor, alacrity, and gratitude. *Raymonda* emerged as a most extraordinary anthology—or procession, if one prefers—of big classic dance pieces, choreographed and staged with exquisite imagination and glittering style.

The subsequent history of Nureyev's *Raymonda,* interesting in itself, provides also an insight into the kind of performance history that most of his restatements of the classic ballets have enjoyed—if, indeed, "enjoyed" is the word one would most accurately choose. In another production a year later, the complete *Raymonda* was given by the Australian Ballet during the course of a British tour. That was in 1965, at the Birmingham Theatre, with Margot Fonteyn and Nureyev dancing the principal roles. The same production was then seen in London, from where it returned to Australia. In 1966, the smaller company of the Royal Ballet, with Fonteyn and Keith Rosson as guest artists, performed Nureyev's choreographic version of the third act only, at the Helsinki Opera House, with new scenery and costumes by the Australian designer, Barry Kay. Two years later, still 1968, the same third act, with scenery by Ralph Koltai, was included in the repertory of the Norwegian Ballet. Only in 1969 did the main company of the Royal Ballet offer an expanded version of Nureyev's third act at the Royal Opera House, Covent Garden. On that occasion, Svetlana Beriosova, partnered by Donald MacLeary, danced the role of Raymonda.

In his production of the complete *Raymonda* for American Ballet Theatre, 1975.
Photograph by Beverley Gallegos.

In *Raymonda.* Photograph by Judy Cameron.

Nureyev maintained his conviction of the merit of the full-length ballet, and in 1972, commissioned Nicholas Georgiadis to design new scenery and costumes for still another mounting of the complete work, which he was preparing for the Ballet of the Zurich Opera House, a production in which he was to appear opposite Marcia Haydée. It was this version that was staged by American Ballet Theatre, with Nureyev, Cynthia Gregory, and Erik Bruhn. First performed at the Jones Hall in Houston, Texas in 1975, it was seen at the New York State Theater in the summer of that year, and subsequently presented, in an unusual, extended run, at the Uris Theatre on Broadway.

This spasmodic performance history of Nureyev's *Raymonda* tells us a good deal about the manner in which his productions have been mounted and treated. Only rarely have they become standard repertory items. There have been exceptions, of course: his Vienna *Swan Lake*; his stagings of *The Sleeping Beauty* for the National Ballet of Canada and for London Festival Ballet. Yet, for the most part, these productions have been conceived by the companies—perhaps with Nureyev's acquiescence—primarily as vehicles for the dancer himself rather than as permanent acquisitions and additions to the repertory of the company. Of course, if Nureyev were present to dance it, a production such as *The Sleeping Beauty* which

he mounted for Milan's La Scala would surely be revived. But in the main, very few companies seem to have drawn on the Nureyev repertory as a source of permanent choreographic enrichment. This is unfortunate, and it is particularly unfortunate in the instance of the Royal Ballet, the company with which he was most identified in Europe.

Swan Lake was the next work in the classical repertory to which Nureyev turned his attention. He had already been associated with the earlier Robert Helpmann production at Covent Garden, to which he had interpolated a first act solo—which quickly became standard—as well as the polonaise and mazurka. Margot Fonteyn joined him in the new version made for the Vienna State Opera Ballet in 1964. Nureyev's *Swan Lake* was not one of his most successful mountings of a classic work. Although it displayed interesting aspects—particularly a male variation danced to the pas de deux coda in the second act—it was somewhat wanting in authority and choreographic or dramatic distinction. Still, it offered him an even more demanding challenge than he had hitherto accepted. Paired with his arresting *Tancredi*—Nureyev's first totally original ballet—his *Swan Lake* intimated something of what he might one day do, and very differently, with that traditional *Swan Lake* as more or less the same kind of man—an outsider, the neurotic male animal frenetically attempting to come to terms with his environment—announced the presence of a notable intellectual dramaturgy.

American Ballet Theatre 40th Anniversary Gala, May 4, 1980: Leon Danielian, Nora Kaye, Ivan Nagy, Irina Baronova, Kevin McKenzie, Antony Tudor, Natalia Makarova, Erik Bruhn, Carla Fracci, Nureyev, Dennis Nahat, Yoko Morishita, Marianna Tcherkassky, and Martine van Hamel. Photograph by J. Oghidanian.

With Cynthia Gregory in *Raymonda* for American Ballet Theatre, 1975.
Photograph by Beverley Gallegos.

Nureyev's next foray into the classical heritage, also at the invitation of the Vienna State Opera, was a new version of the Petipa *Don Quixote.* Although employing the original Ludwig Minkus score, Nureyev engaged John Lanchbery to arrange and orchestrate the complete ballet as well as to make several additions. I did not have the opportunity to see this 1966 Viennese version, but reports on it were not entirely gratifying. Even so, it may well have been Nureyev's most ambitious undertaking at that point. It seems to have served admirably as a first draft for the *Don Quixote* he was to stage in 1970 for the Australian Ballet, with himself as Basilio, Lucette Aldous as Kitri, and Robert Helpmann as the Don. In line with Nureyev's customary procedure, even this was something in the nature of a work in progress. When he reproduced the work for the Ballet of the Marseille Opéra House—again with Aldous, Helpmann, and himself in the principal roles—he seized the occasion to make substantial changes in the production and choreography. The Australian Ballet incorporated those alterations in the version it offered in Sydney in 1972. At last, Nureyev seemed satisfied with the standard of this *Don Quixote,* and he permitted it to be used as the basis for his exhilarating and well-known film version of the ballet which he co-directed. Later he staged the complete *Don Quixote* in Oslo for the Norwegian Ballet, with interesting new scenery and costumes by Nadine Baylis, and finally in 1982 reverting to the earlier Nicholas Georgiadis designs, he presented it with the Boston Ballet in Boston and on extensive tours.

Of all Nureyev's ventures into the full-length classical repertory, three have attained major international eminence, representing the most important body of his choreographic enterprise to date—his versions of *The Sleeping Beauty, The Nutcracker,* and, in rather a slightly different fashion, his more recent production of *Romeo and Juliet.*

The Sleeping Beauty is, of course, the most traditional. The Royal Ballet's version of the work had been part of his aesthetic introduction to the West, just as his memories of and experience in the Konstantin Sergeyev mounting for the Kirov Company constituted a significant part of his Soviet heritage. In September, 1966 when Nureyev set out to stage the ballet, with Carla Fracci as his Aurora, he was probably most influenced by the Kirov production. Although he maintained certain set elements of the classic 1890 Petipa version—the Rose Adagio, the Fairy Variations in the Prologue, the two great pas de deux in the last act—Nureyev made no marked effort to reproduce in detail either the Kirov choreography or the more faithful Petipa reconstruction favored by the Royal Ballet. For the most part, he improvised choreography that was tactfully based on remembrance of the past, translated with taste into Nureyev's view of the present. He offered the cogent production of a fairy tale, stylistically congruent not only with the Tchaikovsky music, but just as important, with the original St. Petersburg ideal of grandeur and simplicity.

With Lucette Aldous in his production of *Don Quixote* for the Australian Ballet, New York, 1970.
Photograph by Dina Makarova.

As might have been predicted, Nureyev's version of *The Sleeping Beauty* also provided the role of the Prince with more opportunities for dancing than most previous stagings of the ballet had done. Nureyev recognized clearly the failure of earlier productions of the Maryinsky classic to exploit the possibilities of the male dancer, and he knew the sources of that curious vacuum: how Petipa and Ivanov, in Petersburg at the end of the nineteenth century, faced a situation in which interest centered almost exclusively on the ballerina, despite the presence of admirable male dancers. (Nijinsky himself was practically waiting in the wings, or at least in the school.) Yet the *premier danseur* roles were still dominated by the venerable but aging Pavel Gerdt, and in consequence, the amount of actual dancing accorded these princely figures was appropriately small.

At that time, the tradition was to give the secondary dancers the solo parts. . .that's why Nijinsky did lot of solos. . . Fokine started with Pavillon d'Armide, *still it was a secondary part, slave. . .and then Fokine discovered those peculiar talents of Nijinsky and he creates the real Nijinsky, and discovers, sees his potential: because of Fokine, Nijinsky blossoms and blossoms to whatever he is. . .*

Nureyev altered all that—not only by amplifying the sheer volume of dancing allotted to the Prince, but by executing those enhanced occasions for display with his uniquely appealing blend of slightly supercilious insolence and radiant charm. His very entrance suggested a young man out of Vermeer painting. And no other dancer presents so sharply defined a persona on stage as he—even his walk could almost be copyrighted. He had a style of bearing, and a sheer technical aplomb that was almost dangerous in its accuracy. He set a style for dance that virtually beggars description.

Nureyev's version of *The Sleeping Beauty* proved so successful and popular that he decided to reproduce it elsewhere. In 1972 he mounted it for the National Ballet of Canada with scenery and costumes by Nicholas Georgiadis that offered a slight variation on the original La Scala designs. This production, which was subsequently filmed for television, is now a standard work in the repertory of that Company, and one of its most popular attractions. Three years later, in 1975, he staged much the same production for the British public, but not at the invitation of the Royal Ballet. It was the London Festival Ballet that was host to Nureyev on this occasion, and there too, as with the National Ballet of Canada, the work has become a permanent acquisition of the Festival repertory. Imaginative and stylish, inventive yet faithful in its fashion to the Petipa original, Nureyev's version of *The Sleeping Beauty* is now generally acknowledged as a remarkable theatrical enterprise, accurate in its vision and essence, and offering an experience of the ballet that is simple, direct, and often powerful. In 1981 he mounted *The Sleeping Beauty* for the Vienna State Opera Ballet.

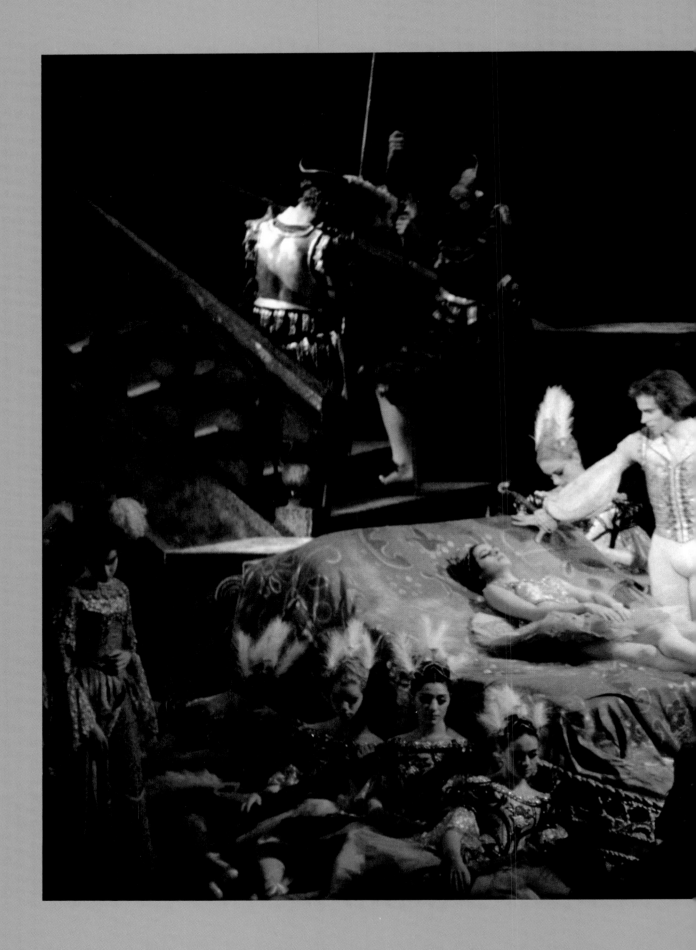

Nureyev's version of *The Nutcracker* is without question the most radical of the major classical reconstructions he has undertaken thus far. To date, he has mounted five different productions of this ballet, all generically the same, but each exhibiting a slight revision or mutation of its predecessor. *The Nutcracker* offers peculiar difficulties to anyone venturesome enough to attempt its staging. The original Petipa and Ivanov choreography seems to have been abandoned entirely, despite the preservation of parts of it by the Royal Ballet well into the forties. Companies all over the world produce it now with scant regard for historical accuracy, and even George Balanchine's celebrated version of it for the New York City Ballet, although largely traditional, employs new choreography.

The principal difficulty of this child's dream of Christmas is that the scenario of *The Nutcracker* makes very little dramatic sense. Clara, the ostensible heroine, is a mime part for a child, and the ballerina and the premier danseur do not emerge until the second act. This division reduces considerably the possibility of a cogent human interest, and even of a certain human sensibility itself. In 1934 the Soviet choreographer, Vassily Vainonen, made perhaps the first concerted effort to resolve the crucial dramatic problem of *The Nutcracker*.

With Karen Kain in his production of *The Sleeping Beauty* for the National Ballet of Canada, 1976. Photograph by Leslie E. Spatt.

Fundamentally, his solution turned on persuading the audience to see in the Sugar Plum Fairy of the last act the personification of Clara in the first act.

Vainonen's stroke of identification set the pattern for most subsequent productions of *The Nutcracker*, and it was natural—in the light of Nureyev's Soviet legacy—that he would draw on Vainonen's inspiration when he turned his own attention to the ballet. Here again, Clara and the Sugar Plum Fairy made a dramatic continuity, but Nureyev sought to explore more penetratingly the psychic ambiguities and implications of *The Nutcracker*. He reverted to the original E.T.A. Hoffmann tale, and attempted in his stagecraft to evoke the looming gothic atmosphere that enfolds Hoffmann's original story. He was alert at once to the potentialities for menace and fantasy in the enigmatic figure of Dr. Drosselmeyer, the macabre presence who stalks through the first act—that otherwise benign scene of the children's party—and indeed is the guest who gives to Clara the Nutcracker Doll. In every production of the work, Drosselmeyer is endowed to some extent with magical propensities, but Nureyev invested him with darker Freudian intimations of paternal authority, preparing us for the inevitable transformation of the sinister old man of the ballet's opening into the Prince of Clara's dreams—with Clara, of course, as his chosen Princess. The motif of Drosselmeyer's actual translation into the glittering Prince of fantasy, with all its rich store of psychic and emotional implication, was unique to Nureyev's conception, wholly of his own devising.

The opportunity to mount *The Nutcracker* was first offered by Erik Bruhn, who invited Nureyev to prepare it for the Royal Swedish Ballet at a time in 1967, when Bruhn was that Company's artistic director. Its premiere was on November 17th of that year at the Royal Theatre, Stockholm, with Mariane Orlando as Clara and Caj Selling in the dual role of Drosselmeyer and the Prince. It was always intended that his production should be, to some degree, a preview of the Royal Ballet production scheduled for London in February of the following year. With new scenery and costumes commissioned from Nicholas Georgiadis, that version was offered at the Royal Opera House, Covent Garden, on February 29, 1968. Merle Park danced Clara and Nureyev himself appeared in his own conception of Drosselmeyer and the Prince. Although the substance of the production remained intact, Nureyev continued to make revisions in both the choreography and the design throughout subsequent versions presented at La Scala in Milan, at the Teatro Colón in Buenos Aires, and again at Covent Garden. New York first saw Nureyev's interpretation of *The Nutcracker* during the course of the 1970 tour of the Royal Ballet, and in 1980 he presented it again, this time with the Berlin Ballet.

In its mature dramatic complexity, its choreographic freedom, and—perhaps most

Rehearsing his production of *The Nutcracker*, Royal Ballet, 1968. Photograph by Reg Wilson.

important—the sense it subtly conveyed of a fresh capacity to transcend the familiar if venerable hallmarks of the Petipa and Soviet stylistic models, this restatement of *The Nutcracker* marked a formidable advance in Nureyev's powers. It also confirmed—in its dance invention (particularly in the second act pas de deux), as well as its skill in delineating atmosphere and evoking the sense of a distant place and time—the legitimacy of Nureyev's claim to be regarded as a significant new force in the realm of ballet innovation. No version of *The Nutcracker* that we have ever seen has been more potently dramatic; few have displayed so sharp an imprint of personal style.

Drama and style have been heightened to even a more intense pitch in what is Nureyev's most elaborate choreographic achievement so far, the full-length staging of Prokofiev's ballet *Romeo and Juliet*.

Nureyev's involvement with the substance of Shakespeare's doomed lovers had been, of course, a major element in the history of his dance presence ever since he first appeared as Romeo in Kenneth MacMillan's version of the work, mounted for the Royal Ballet on February 9, 1965. It is generally, and correctly, regarded as one of his signature roles.

To be sure, the stuff of *Romeo and Juliet* was a notable part of his Soviet legacy. As a student in Leningrad, he had been well-acquainted with the celebrated production Leonid Lavrovsky originated for the Bolshoi Theater. Clearly, this masterly version worthy of Fokine, was to leave a lasting impression on him, but Nureyev always felt somehow that in its nature and sensibility—the parade of Renaissance arts and attitudes it offered—the work was more Italianate than Shakespearean. In time, he was to be exposed to other choreographic restatements of the fate of the lovers of Verona: the fluent approach, after Petipa, as it were, taken by Frederick Ashton in his version for the Royal Danish Ballet; the sturdy and turbulent production that is a major attraction of John Cranko's Stuttgart company; even an abstract account of the work arranged by Rudi van Dantzig for his own Dutch National Ballet.

Nureyev—as well as Fonteyn—had been most closely identified with the MacMillan version of the ballet which, like the Cranko before it—to which it bears a striking similarity—represents something of a rapprochement between the formal dramatic spectacle offered by Lavrovsky and the tasteful classical reserve that marked Ashton's approach. All of these individual attitudes, memories, and sensibilities were available to Nureyev's imagination when the London Festival Ballet commissioned him to choreograph and stage a new production of *Romeo and Juliet* to be the highlight of their 1977 Australian tour, with Nureyev as principal guest artist. What Nureyev took as his goal was a version profoundly more Shakespearean in essence and spirit than any of its predecessors—one, too, that would place Shakespeare and his young Veronese lovers in their proper context of Renaissance life and fate.

It is appropriate to observe here that Nureyev, perhaps more than any other contemporary choreographer, is avid in his attention to the theater and films, and it would come as no surprise that his choreographic approach should inevitably be colored by his intense regard for theater as theater. Equally, he is a classical master *par excellence,* and his reverence for the technique, the craft, the traditions of his school, is absolutely boundless. He came at this *Romeo and Juliet,* then, by immersing himself first in the play, but equally in histories and pictorial representations of the Italy in which Shakespeare set his romantic tragedy. Not only did he search the play and its world, he submitted his imagination to the implications of Shakespeare's conception and thought and his approach to these particular characters. What he emerged with was a passionate and full-bodied Elizabethan ritual, far more potent than most of its antecedents, and, however disconcerting to some, aflame with the dramatic urgency and thrust that Nureyev had captured first in its original scenario and subsequently in the choreographic treatment of the substance.

In his production of *The Nutcracker,* Royal Ballet, 1968. Photograph by Reg Wilson/Camera Press, Ltd.

With designs by Ezio Frigerio and lighting by Tharon Musser, Nureyev's production of *Romeo and Juliet* was given its premiere by the London Festival Ballet on June 2, 1977 at the London Coliseum. Nureyev himself appeared as the ballet's first Romeo, to the Juliet of Patricia Ruanne. The remainder of the cast included Manola Asensio as Rosaline, Jonas Kage as Benvolio, Nicholas Johnson as Mercutio, Frederic Werner as Tybalt, Alain Dubreuil as Paris, Elizabeth Anderton as the nurse, and Valerie Aitkin and Terry Hayworth as Lord and Lady Capulet.

In talking with Nureyev as he was about to start rehearsals, and later on viewing the ballet, I was struck by the thoroughness with which he had absorbed—even saturated himself in—the Shakespeare text. I noted, too, the deliberateness with which he placed a private domestic drama squarely within the context of a savage, brutal, and squalid time. He introduced a number of signal innovations. For example, he included a brief prologue in which we see four hooded figures casting dice—patently a reference to what Nureyev felt was one of the prime motifs of the play: chance. This scene was followed instantly by the spectacle of a grisly tumbrel carting dead bodies across the stage—an intimation that the Black Death or some other terrible affliction had struck Verona. Whether these images and elements are to be found in Shakespeare's text, they embody a visually poetic extension of Elizabethan sensibility that is dramatically quite defensible.

Nureyev stressed the life and destiny of *all* participants. He presented a world in which the personages are markedly younger than is the custom when the play, as well as its balletic version, is produced. All his young people are scarcely more than adolescent; his Lady Capulet is evidently a woman in her mid-thirties; even the nurse is not the familiar antique butt of doddering humor. He sees both Romeo and Juliet as essentially headstrong, and in Nureyev's version it is Juliet—even more than her young lover—who seizes the initiative. In his own dancing, which had an air of destiny to it—gestures shaping the air into ineffable poetry—he conveyed the drama's flare of brightness and gaiety as well as its eruptions of reckless violence and sudden death.

In choreographic style, Nureyev seems to owe almost nothing to his predecessors. For the most part he has scrupulously avoided the two versions—the British and the Soviet—that he personally knew. The clowns and lute players in the market scene are, for instance, gone, replaced by acrobats who indulge in the ancient Sienese (well, Siena is not Verona, but it is not far away) art of flag throwing.

Nureyev also goes to pains to build up characters other than the star-cross'd lovers. Mercutio becomes a role almost as important as Romeo's own. Benvolio, who has a duet with Romeo in Mantua, is also emphasized. Tybalt is made gentler.

The sensitive settings of the Italian designer, Ezio Frigerio, rather better known in opera than in ballet, created a real and sunlit world for the choreographer's imagination to inhabit. The thoughtful yet passionate understatement of these designs is beautifully in accord with the choreographer's concept. Some of Nureyev's choreography was criticized for its lack of imagination, or inventiveness, and this may have been true of the love duets. But his major concern here was hardly inventiveness. What he sought to do was to present a vision of what has been called "the Elizabethan World Picture"—a frame for the dramatic story of two lovers and their tragic fate—and in realizing that intention, he has been abundantly successful.

Nureyev's original ballet *Romeo and Juliet* gives us Shakespeare come to dance with a most extraordinary authority and power. In 1977 this production for the London Festival Ballet received the Society of West End Theatres Award for *outstanding achievement for the year in ballet.*

With Margot Fonteyn and Carla Fracci after a performance of his original ballet, *Romeo and Juliet*, La Scala Opera Ballet, New York, 1981. Photograph by Jack Vartoogian.

Much has been written of Rudolf Nureyev as a dancer—understandably so. Since he burst on the Western world that summer of 1961 it is conceivable that he has danced more often and before more people than any other dancer in the world. He has filled column inches of the world press as if he were a political leader. Words, words, words. Some of them are in interviews, some enshrined in feature articles, some merely decorating the fluffy, often inaccurate gossip columns.

What dance historians, equipped with computers and text withdrawal systems we cannot quite envisage, will make of all this verbal overkill one must not imagine. Think of all those buttons being pressed in antiseptic campus libraries, and the dozens, perhaps hundreds, of Ph.D. theses being launched. Yet what these brave historians might be surprised to discover is that despite this mountain of critical gristle, journalistic flesh, and media fluff, comparatively little has been written about what will probably prove to be the most enduring aspect of his career—namely, the influence he has exerted on twentieth century ballet.

With Charlene Gehn, and Bonnie Wyckoff in Vaslav Nijinsky's *L'Après-midi d'un Faune*, Joffrey Ballet, New York, 1979. Photograph by Lois Greenfield.

Obviously, ballet in the United States and the entire world would have been very different if Nureyev had not existed. Yet this influence is not always easy to trace or pin down. For example we now talk freely of the dance explosion, its causes and effects. Those causes are complex, indeed, and it could be that a social historian of the future will determine that the prime cause was the proliferation of television, producing people more susceptible to the visual image than the written or spoken word. Among the other factors must surely be placed the emergence of the ballet superstars. Despite the widespread popularity of such dancers even in this century as Anna Pavlova, the first true superstars, backed up the publicity mechanics and the media exposure unavailable until the mid-twentieth century, were in that remarkable partnership of Margot Fonteyn and Rudolf Nureyev. While the impact of Nureyev's individual fame—particularly together with Fonteyn's—certainly played its role in ballet's soaring popularity, this is still the least, the most ephemeral, of Nureyev's contributions to the art.

Where his force has been most significantly felt is in his example as a dancer and a coach, and, later, his influence as a director and choreographer. In many ways Nureyev has changed the face of ballet. The features he perhaps changed most were those of Britain's Royal Ballet—his first real company in the West. He had an enormous effect upon the Royal Ballet, an effect that can still be felt today. At first he was resented; it took Nureyev a long time to win acceptance. He was not particularly easy to work with. The effect he started to have on the company—particularly the male dancers, was incredible. A few dropped out, unfortunately, and a few careers were bruised, but the younger dancers got the message. I firmly believe that Anthony Dowell and David Wall (who was only in the School when Nureyev arrived) to take only two instances, would have developed quite differently had it not been for Nureyev's presence.

Nureyev's presence influenced the careers of many young dancers, inspiring them to aspire to his skills and artistry. Revealingly, he has always been generous with his coaching and advice.

Like the student Trofimov who says: "I am not the one who is going to redo society, but I am going to show them where it is, which way to go."

Reaching for something, because reaching for something rather than telling, for me is more important.

He has also made his influence felt through ballet companies themselves. He has made possible enhanced touring opportunities for many of the companies he has danced with. At times his activities in this direction have proved controversial.

Nureyev's presence has acted as a stimulus to many companies ranging from the Murray

In the *La Sylphide* segment of the film *I Am a Dancer*, 1972. Photograph by Serge Lido.

In Erik Bruhn's production of Bournonville's *La Sylphide* for National Ballet of Canada, 1972.
Photograph by Judy Cameron.

Louis Dance Company to London Festival Ballet, from the Martha Graham Company to the Dutch National Ballet, from the Australian Ballet and the National Ballet of Canada to the Joffrey Ballet, from the Paul Taylor Company to the Berlin Ballet, La Scala Opera Ballet, Zurich Opera Ballet, or the Boston Ballet, with whom in New York he gave the American premiere of Pierre Lacotte's sensitive and sensible reconstruction of Filippo Taglioni's original *La Sylphide.*

To these companies, some of whom have really only been able to appear in London or New York clinging to his coat-tails, he appears to have given a great deal, if only in visibility. His shrewd manager, Sandor Gorlinsky, his usual American impresario James Nederlander, head of the theater chain, the Metropolitan Opera Management, and his British impresario, Victor Hochhauser, seem to have managed to set their star against a backdrop of more or less distinguished companies.

These backdrop companies have obviously benefitted not only financially, and Nureyev has also emerged ahead of the game. Murray Louis and the Netherlands National Ballet have provided him with interesting, challenging new roles, as has Martha Graham. The Joffrey Ballet gave him the opportunity to dance Nijinsky's *L'Après-Midi d'un Faune* in a scrupulously careful reproduction, which he was later to repeat, along with his performances in *Le Spectre de la Rose* and *Petrushka* on nationwide television.

Nureyev's dancing as Nijinsky's Faune was remarkable. The designer-consultant for the season, Rouben Ter-Arutunian went to every effort to ensure that the Bakst setting and costumes would be totally authentic. Joffrey himself, a stickler for tradition, who loves ballets past almost as much as ballets future, helped arrange for Elizabeth Schooling and William Chappell (who had learned the ballet from Marie Rambert) to teach it to Nureyev and the company. The result was a performance of *Faune* totally unequalled since Rambert herself taught the role to Nureyev's great predecessor, Jean Babilée in 1949.

Nureyev's sinuous and sensuous dancing did give one a backward glimpse of what Nijinsky—nowadays only seen with the vividness of remembered photographs, snap-shots of a murky history—must have been like. Nureyev's Golden Slave was less successful—but that was a role that was probably less successful for Nijinsky as well; we have it on record that he often preferred to dance the Chief Eunuch, sending in the unannounced Alexandre Gavrilov as the Golden Slave.

However as the Spectre, Nureyev was once again meeting the ineffable, invisible and lost image of Nijinsky. How did he compare? I seriously doubt whether there are more than a thousand persons alive today who actually saw Nijinsky dance. And I would hesitate to suggest how large a handful of that thousand also saw Nureyev. Yet throughout his career

In *Vivace,* choreographed on Nureyev by Murray Louis, 1978. Photograph by Zoë Dominic.   205

he, and possibly to some extent his fellow Kirov expatriate, Mikhail Baryshnikov, have always had to measure up to the Nijinsky dance legend that has become a dance myth.

I have seen many great dancers attempt *Spectre*—a very young Erik Bruhn, Babilée, of course, John Gilpin, coached by Karsavina herself, and Baryshnikov, cling to the memory— and by the time Nureyev came to the role he never quite had the jump. But what was fantastic was the realization of Nijinsky's strangely orientalized *ports de bras*. These arm movements have to flow like an art nouveau painting. You can see it in the handsomely documented Nijinsky photographs. And it was this melting quality—it is the quality that gives the role its Aubrey Beardsley senses of sexual ambiguity—that Nureyev so triumphantly perceived, developed, and displayed.

Nureyev takes almost as much as he gives. He had danced James in Bournonville's *La Sylphide* around the world, chiefly in the Erik Bruhn production for the National Ballet of Canada. Yet he jumped at the chance to do the Lacotte/Taglioni reconstruction, first given for the Paris Opéra, with the Boston Ballet. It was a different challenge. Choreographically, of course, the Lacotte version is no match for Bournonville's Danish original, one of the very oldest consistently maintained ballets in the repertory. Nevertheless, with its hero having more aristocratic leanings than Bournonville's peasant-laird, and a different approach, both choreographically and, even more, dramatically, Nureyev clearly sensed a chance for expansion. When he returns to the Bournonville, as he must, one knows that some dust from this Lacotte experiment will have touched him, and his performance.

After his productive years with the Royal Ballet, Nureyev has become a nomad. Yet he is a nomad possessing unusual roots. Rather like Balanchine, he has some tiny classroom at the Maryinsky School locked in his head as, if nothing more, a symbol of excellence. He will dance virtually anything for a new experience—some new awakening of the muscles—but his standards are strict and impeccable.

His recent appearances are generally either in classics, often those he has staged himself, with backdrops, or, less frequently of late, with a dozen or so dancers, one or two well-known, in a program generically called *Nureyev and Friends.* It has given him opportunities. He has loped winningly through Paul Taylor's *Aureole,* and looked tensely, but interestingly classical, in Balanchine's *Apollo.*

Occasionally the nomad is pushed further than you might expect. In 1980 the Berlin Ballet came to the Metropolitan Opera House, with Nureyev as a guest artist. For Nureyev perhaps the major attraction was a revival of his remarkable and singular *Nutcracker*—the Royal Ballet gave Berlin the sets and costumes—and the opportunity to play once more that strange, yet totally convincing, personage, the dichotymous Drosselmeyer/Prince, a combination that even Freud would have called Freudian.

In *Moment,* choreographed on Nureyev by Murray Louis in 1975. Photograph by Beverley Gallegos.

208   With Karen Kain, Paolo Bortoluzzi, and Margot Fonteyn in José Limón's *The Moor's Pavane,*
"Nureyev and Friends," Washington, 1975. Photograph by Louis Péres.

With Anne Marie Vessel in Flemming Flindt's *The Lesson,* "Nureyev and Friends," New York, 1975.   209
Photograph by Beverley Gallegos.

Yet, as part of the package that companies make on these strange commercial occasions, he also danced Prince Myshkin in Valery Panov's hysterically and histrionically dramatic, full-evening ballet based on Dostoievsky's *The Idiot*.

Panov had mounted the role of Myshkin on another Russian émigré, Vladimir Gelvan, who alternated in the role during the New York season. In some ways, technically, for example, Gelvan was better. But in the final accounting there could be no choice. Nureyev was a Myshkin that, at that moment in time, only Anthony Dowell and Mikhail Baryshnikov might possibly have matched. The role demanded a great dance actor, and through

With Valery Panov in Panov's *The Idiot* for the Berlin Ballet, New York, 1980.
Photograph by Beverley Gallegos.

Rehearsing the final moment in *The Idiot*. Photograph by Louis Péres.

the perspective of Nureyev's success with it, one could see how far he had advanced as a dramatic personality over two decades.

He was so subtle. He walked through the ballet like a truly innocent child of God. His dancing was fine. Pitted against Panov, dancing Rogozhin, he danced his duet duel with handsome expertise. But this was not important—well, at least, this was not significant. What impressed me was his ability to strike to the heart of Dostoievsky.

Previously I had seen two really masterful realizations of Myshkin. One was Gérard Philipe in a French movie, and the other, on stage, was the great Innokenti Smoklovsky in Leningrad. Nureyev, with his pleading eyes and soft gestures, his mysterious presence, Myshkin's white-on-white visibility, matched—even combined—both of them. Philipe was all passion, the lover, whereas Smoklovsky was all innocence, the fool. Both overlapped each other's performance, and it was in that overlapping that Nureyev lived.

How good an actor, outside the confines of ballet, is he? Immediately before I wrote this, I watched him again on tape in Ken Russell's *Valentino*. The film was a disaster from the first take, because Russell had no interest in who Valentino was, and was only fascinated in mimicking, that silver and silent screen, now brought to you in living talking color.

It was a shabby movie that exploited Nureyev as if he were a product rather than a person. However, it has one scene worth your attention, and so far as Nureyev was concerned—perhaps the most effective part of the Valentino film came when he did a top-hat, white tie, and tails number a la Fred Astaire. Nureyev, alias Valentino, had been hired as a dance gigolo—he danced his way out of the dime a dance cafe where he was meant to be entertaining the people, after having insulted them and been fired. His exit is a gem of dance acting—insolent yet insouciant. Nureyev's idol, Fred Astaire, could not have handled it with more carefree class. There was also a memorable occasion when he appeared on the *Muppets* show and revealed a tremendous amount of ease, charm, and genuine wit as he wowed Miss Piggy, but also produced a beautiful top hat, white tie, and tails number, that was as sleek as it was slick. Nureyev's flirtations with pop are by no means finished, and might one day find a surprising consummation.

Also one must not disregard his aspirations not simply as a mounter of classical ballets, but also as an original choreographer. This career started, as I noted earlier, in 1966 for the Vienna Opera Ballet with a specially commissioned score by Hans Werner Henze. Apart from *Romeo and Juliet*, it was not until 1980 that he took up the challenge once more—when he created a ballet to Tchaikovsky music, based on Byron's *Manfred*.

This was intended to come to New York in the summer of 1980, when the Paris Opéra Ballet was destined to make its first appearance in New York since 1948. Interestingly, even

In Ken Russell's film *Valentino*, 1977. Photograph by United Artists Corporation.

With Kermit the Frog and Miss Piggy during his appearance on *The Muppet Show*, 1978. Photograph by CBS/Gamma.

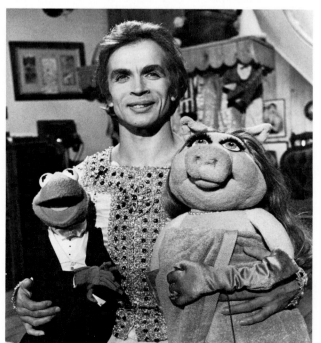

213

ironically, the Paris company refused to appear in New York with guest stars, so the Paris Opéra Ballet and *Manfred* were not seen in New York. Balanchine considered it for his 1981 Tchaikovsky Festival for New York City Ballet, but eventually rejected it.

Expecting to see *Manfred* in New York I did not fly to Paris to see it, so I am at the mercy of the opinion of friends and strangers. However a friend whose opinion I take very seriously is John Percival, a life-long colleague, who succeeded me as dance critic of *The Times* of London. He wrote, in part: "In structure and content, the ballet is a revival of a form once immensely popular but not much practiced lately: what used to be called the symphonic ballet.

"Besides its hero and ten other soloists, the ballet uses an ensemble of about fifty dancers, many of whom appear in different guises from one movement to another.

"The most interesting choreography for the *corps de ballet* as mountain spirits, is in the

214 With Dominique Khalfouni in Nureyev's original ballet, *Manfred,* for the Paris Opera Ballet, 1979. Photograph by Colette Masson.

second scene. Nureyev has always challenged his group dancers with difficult, inventive sequences. Here they have intricate classical dances, largely arranged for seven trios swirling round the stage: tricky, but light, bright and successful."

Some of the other notices were less agreeable, but it does seem entirely possible that Nureyev will wish to branch out more and more as an original choreographer.

One can hardly be as interested in movies, theater and, for that matter dance itself, as Nureyev is, without one day wishing to paddle in the mainstream of creative choreography. *Tancredi, Romeo and Juliet,* and *Manfred,* I am almost certain, are merely harbingers of Nureyev's creative future. And there is also no doubt that as a catalyst for dancers, choreographers, companies, and audiences, Nureyev has already rendered unequalled service in the dance world. It may still be that his most profound influence lies somewhere else; it may also be that his most important contribution remains to be made.

As Manfred. Photograph by Colette Masson.

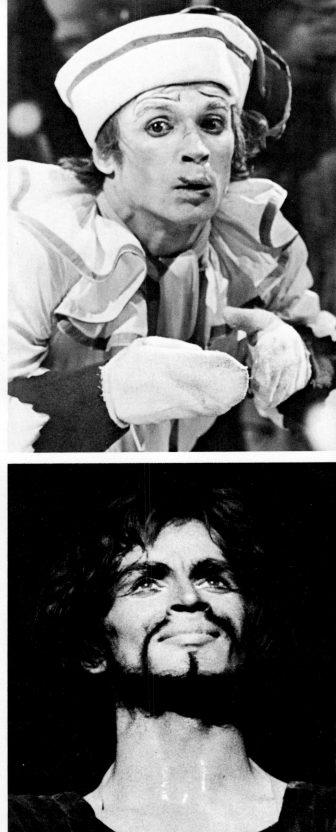

216   In character: left, as the Golden Slave in Michel Fokine's *Schéhérazade*, London Festival Ballet, 1979.
Photograph by Beverley Gallegos. Above, in Michel Fokine's *Petrushka*, Paris, 1976. Photograph by
Colette Masson. Right, as the Moor in José Limón's *The Moor's Pavane*. Photograph by Beverley Gallegos.

Above, in John Neumeier's *Don Juan* for National Ballet of Canada, 1974. Photograph by Ken Bell.   217
Left, in Frederick Ashton's *Marguerite and Armand*, Royal Ballet. Photograph by Roy Round.
Right, in Fokine's *Le Spectre de la Rose*, London Festival Ballet, 1979. Photograph by Beverley Gallegos.

LOOKING AHEAD

It is clear that Nureyev now over forty is not going to be able to maintain the marathon pace that he has kept up for the last twenty years. This is partly a question of pure physical skills, partly a question of physical stamina. One of the saddest aspects of any dancer's career is that at an age when a conductor, or a violinist, or a pianist, even an actor, would still be regarded as young, the dancer is regarded as beyond his or her peak. It is as though a violinist were to be given a Stradivarius, and every year after say thirty-five someone came along and chipped away a little of that Stradivarius. For a time, of course, increasing artistry makes up the difference. And then eventually, inevitably, there comes a point—with each individual dancer this point can vary considerably—where the ascending line of artistry transects the declining line of pure brute energy. At that point of crossing, the dancer is conceivably at his career best. But it is a best that will have no return.

There are many options open to the dancer. For one, he can do as Erik Bruhn once did, find himself a completely new repertory in which he will not be competing with his former self, a repertory that will offer him new artistic challenges, and will enable him to appear without being a shadow for the audience that knew him, and a disappointment to the audience that had only read about him. Of course many dancers do elect to give up dancing altogether and start teaching, choreographing, directing companies, or leave the field completely and enter a related field such as acting or even find themselves a totally new career outside the performing arts. It is inconceivable for anyone to imagine Nureyev outside dance. He is a man who lives dance, breathes dance; dance is to him what oxygen is to anyone else. Although he is a better balanced artist than most of his colleagues and peers, he knows much more about the theater, much more about movies, much more about music and books than almost any of his contemporaries, it does seem that dance itself, the physical joy of dancing, and the possibilities of the total dance experience seem to be the key factor of his career, even the key factor of his entire life.

Always on the go. Photograph by Garofalo/Paris Match.

One might expect the obvious options open to Nureyev to be taken. It is unthinkable that given reasonably good health he would not in some capacity be on stage in twenty, thirty years time. He enjoys the whole business of stage craft, he enjoys making up, he enjoys appearing in front of people, he enjoys the whole ritual of the curtain call, a ritual which he has made so much his own. It is unthinkable that he will not find some way to appear with a company. Perhaps the Albrecht of today will become the Hilarion of tomorrow, perhaps even the Prince of Courland, but it is unthinkable that this intensely theatrical individual will not wish to exercise his craft, will not wish to continue his magic, and not wish to almost feed his habit as a consummate performer. His still evident joy in performing revealed itself very clearly in the spring of 1982 when, after a gap of five years, he was invited back to Covent Garden to dance a few performances in *Swan Lake* and in *La Bayadère* with the Royal Ballet. He was almost unnaturally delighted at this prodigal return so enthusiastically received by the public and the press. His performance workload continues to be formidable—indeed immediately after these appearances with the Royal Ballet, he undertook a cross-country American tour with the Boston Ballet, for whom he had mounted his production of *Don Quixote*. During this tour he danced Basilio, the ballet's barber hero, at every single performance, not even missing out on the matinees.

However, despite his continuing zeal for dancing, he does have other options.

One doubts whether he will not wish to be a teacher. Already any dancer who knows him will recognize what a superb coach he is. Even Margot Fonteyn readily admits his uncanny manner of seeing the physical problems of a step, of being able to diagnose with total assurance the style and manner of a performance. Obviously he will be a superb coach and a masterful repetiteur—he is already. Certainly one will expect him to continue to produce versions of the classics; indeed one would expect him to extend the range of classics which he would want to produce. It is certain that he will also wish to venture in the new field of creative choreography.

Nureyev has created only three completely new ballets. Naturally, much of the choreography in any of his classic ballets is original. For example, in his *Sleeping Beauty*, much is indeed Petipa, but much of it is Nureyev working in the style of Petipa. The same was evidently true of his production of *Raymonda*, and any of the other ballets that he has mounted. The whole conceptual difference of a totally new creative ballet is something which Nureyev has rarely encountered. In 1966 he produced his first original ballet, *Tancredi* for the Vienna State Opera. This modern, psychological work, of enormous literary complexity, was sunk almost beneath a sea of symbolism. Difficult and tortuous in its narrative, as well as somewhat muddled in its choreographic outline, the ballet lasted only a few performances, and Nureyev has shown no interest in resucitating it.

Tancredi was meant to be Nutcracker. I had done Swan Lake, *it proved successful for the local ballet. . .and suddenly something arose, and they wanted modern which I never dreamed of doing. . .*

I did not regard it as something extraordinary, it was something I could do. . .a tough nut to crack to go at this. . .I divided the music in equal parts between all the participants, the main characters: Tancredi and Cantilene, and the girl in black, and her father, and so on. I did not have time to establish Tancredi as a character nor did I have time to establish why. . .

In 1979 he was emboldened to try again, and for the Paris Opéra Ballet produced a work based on Byron, called *Manfred.* This was not too well received by the Paris critics, yet Nureyev believes in its revision and survival.

Indeed he did revise *Manfred* in 1981 for the Zurich Ballet, and a year later the Zurich dancers took it to the London Coliseum, as part of Nureyev's long-standing traditional London season. At one time it was also planned to bring *Manfred* to the Metropolitan Opera House in New York in the fall of 1982, with the ballet being specially mounted by the Joffrey Ballet—but at time of writing this seemed to have fallen through. Nevertheless his determination that one day *Manfred* shall be seen in New York is unwavering.

His most significant creative work, so far, has been his version of Prokofiev's *Romeo and Juliet,* produced in 1977 for London Festival Ballet, and in 1981 for La Scala Opera Ballet.

This interest in creating new choreography may or may not become a lasting concern in Nureyev's future career. However in 1982 his interest in original choreography received a considerable boost, when he was invited to create a new ballet for the Royal Ballet at Covent Garden. Scheduled for its premiere on December 2, this is a dance version of Shakespeare's *The Tempest,* based musically on Tchaikovsky's incidental music to the play, together with some additional music taken from the orchestral suites.

Talking with Nureyev in Boston, at the time of his *Don Quixote* production, he obviously viewed this Covent Garden assignment with some apprehension. Indeed, although he grinned through his nerve-ends, at heart he seemed genuinely nervous at the prospect of creating an entirely new ballet for the Royal Ballet. Previously most of his choreographic work has simply involved the restaging of the classics, where at least the general form and dramaturgy are a known constant. And *The Tempest*—interestingly a project once toyed with in 1957 by Sir Frederick Ashton as a vehicle for Fonteyn as Miranda, but Ashton eventually settled on *Ondine,* which was produced a year later—is only Nureyev's fourth completely original ballet.

The project also clearly means a lot to him personally. Although since January, 1982 Nureyev has been an Austrian citizen, London and the Royal Ballet did become in the days of the Fonteyn-Nureyev partnership his spiritual home, and apart from his original *alma mater*, the Kirov Ballet, the Royal Ballet, in some curious sense, appears to remain in his mind as his *home* company. Asked whether he was nervous about *The Tempest*, he replied: "Yes I am scared...maybe, who knows? I won't be able to think of any steps, and I'll just stand there with the dancers...waiting." But even as he said it, one sensed that waiting was not in his temperament. There are also two other elements in his future career likely to assume burgeoning importance.

First there is his obvious desire, sooner or later—and he has already put it off more than once—to direct and control his own ballet company.

222 In January, 1982 Rudolf Nureyev accepted Austrian citizenship. He is shown with L. Gratz, the Mayor of Vienna. Photograph by UDO Schreiber-US Press/Gamma.

I should have done it long time ago with Margot: I should have had a company and mounted these productions...but then those adventures of going from one company to another of enlarging repertoires...if I had stayed with Royal Ballet of course I would not have been exposed to the same adventures...I would not have choreographed so many productions, and maybe I would not have kept myself in that classical shape I keep myself to...All those productions that I mounted in Vienna, Milano, Stockholm, Zurich, in Marseille, Cologne, Buenos Aires, in Canada, for American Ballet Theatre...It's only through those productions that I managed to keep myself....

It is virtually certain that he will either acquire one of the world's great ballet companies, or, conceivably, even have a company built specially for him. This was a possibility that at one time was actively explored by Anthony Bliss, General Manager of the Metropolitan Opera Association and also incidentally Board Chairman of the Joffrey Ballet, to see whether a classic ballet company, performing chiefly the full-length popular classics, could not be formed at the Metropolitan Opera House. However, partly because of the Opera House's improving funding situation, this never-announced proposal has been shelved indefinitely and probably permanently.

Nevertheless, it does appear that in 1983 Nureyev will have his own company—the Paris Opéra Ballet, the oldest of all dance companies, if not, currently, the most distinguished. At time of writing, the actual agreements appear to have been made. Certainly Nureyev takes the offer seriously enough to have acquired a vast new apartment in Paris, on the Quai Voltaire. There is one unusual stipulation that Nureyev is making—and one that certainly means he would not be a passive director. I had asked him whether he would take this Parisian opportunity to retire from dancing, or at least cut down on the number of performances and possibly the type of role played.

Thus questioned whether he would reduce his performing schedule—Nureyev merely looked, amused, suspicious and scoffing—possibly not in that order of emotional precedence. He laughed: "You want me to stop? No, I'd die. My contract with Paris calls for at least thirty performances with the company per season." Anyone who knows Nureyev will recognize what emphasis he places on that "at least."

The second development foreshadowed in his future career will almost certainly be outside dance.

Nureyev is no stranger to the film medium. In addition to frequently appearing as a guest on popular TV talk shows, Nureyev's dancing has been extensively recorded for the screen. From his first appearances on German TV and in 1962 on the Bell Telephone Hour in the United States, Nureyev has starred in ballet films, Kenneth MacMillan's *Romeo and*

Juliet, An Evening with the Royal Ballet, among others, as well as in his own ballet productions, filmed either for TV or for conventional movie theater release. Films such as *Don Quixote* and *I am a Dancer* have been shown periodically over the last decade here and abroad.

Through the made-for-TV programs, including Roland Petit's *Le Jeune Homme et la Mort, Petrushka,* Paul Taylor's *Big Bertha* segment on the *Burt Bacharach Special* on CBS, Birgit Cullberg's *Adam and Eve,* and CBS' *Julie Andrews' Invitation to the Dance,* Nureyev has been able to extend his expression of the modern-dance language.

Nureyev is a consummate movie fan. He goes to the cinema three or four times a week and keeps up with almost every important movie made. While he goes to the theater a great deal—he sees most of the important plays—there is no doubt in my mind that he has a greater affinity for the cinema as a medium than he does for the dramatic theater.

It would be very easy to see him making films, not especially, or not particularly, and certainly not exclusively, ballet films. One can see him experimenting as a director on his own, even experimenting as an actor. Already he has made his film debut as an actor in the rather ill-advised *Valentino.* This film by Ken Russell was by no one's account a particular success. On the other hand, it did show Nureyev as a very powerful film persona, and he had the glamour, the bearing, and that special mark of the film star. Unfortunately neither he nor his director, the idiosyncratic Ken Russell, knew how to translate that persona into the ordinary business of film acting. As a result, he wandered through the film more like an

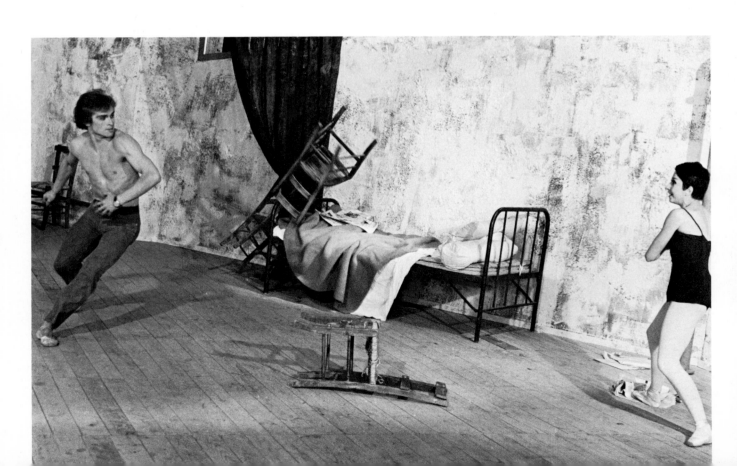

emblem than anything else, continually upsetting the balance of Russell's grotesque fantasy, and never being able to impose on the film his own imprint.

After the box-office failure of *Valentino*, Nureyev was not a so-called "bankable proposition" in Hollywood terms, and an idea being played around with by the director Herbert Ross for some kind of sequel to his movie *The Turning Point* and starring Nureyev, got little further than the eye-gleaming stage. However in 1982 Nureyev made a film called *Exposed*, which was filmed largely in New York, and has Nastassia Kinski as the dancer's co-star. This is strictly a non-dancing role, and Nureyev was far happier with the result than he had ever been with *Valentino*, which had proved a misery even during the shooting.

With Zizi Jeanmaire in Roland Petit's television adaptation of *Le Jeune Homme et la Mort*, Paris, 1966. 225
Photographs by Jürgen Vollmer.

There is also no doubt that he has a considerable interest in the business of film directing. When he made the film of *Don Quixote* with the Australian Ballet, he quickly realized that unless he had control of the cameras as well as control of the dancers, the film would not be his own product. As a result, he very quickly learned as much about the actual business and craft of film directing as he could, and he is accredited, rightly so, as a co-director of this film. Indeed, he was the co-director who was powerfully instrumental in the final shots, also powerfully instrumental in the editing, and he did make this film more than any of his other dance films a product of his individual taste and talent. It is unquestionably the most successful film he has ever made.

In London he also directed a television version of his *Romeo and Juliet.* This video version I have yet to see, but it is said that Nureyev himself had complete control over its taping and was very happy with the results.

Another aspect of his future is quite obviously in modern-dance. He has been carefully preparing himself for this for many years. In part this has been the natural inquisitiveness of wanting to know everything there is to know about the various forms of dance technique. When he first saw Martha Graham dance, when he first saw her company, and when he got to know Paul Taylor he became fascinated by this form of theatrical dancing that was so remote from his own academy, so different from what his muscles knew from kinetic

memory. Nor did he take this up simply as a gifted amateur. He took it extremely seriously. There was none of the feeling that many classic ballet dancers have that any modern steps can be picked up simply by any classically-trained dancer. Nureyev took it much more seriously; he had classes with Graham; he studied the modern dance technique right from the basics. This gave him an authority, particularly perhaps in Graham, that very few classic dancers have ever retained when they moved outside their previously chosen field. Interestingly, with Graham, he became almost more like the older generation of Graham dancers— that generation with the intense conceptual projection of Graham characters—than the younger generation of Graham dancers with whom he was dancing. Whether he will continue his experiments with modern-dance troupes remains to be seen. However, I think it very likely that he may, even while directing his own company, find time to make the occasional foray into modern-dance with such troupes as Paul Taylor, Murray Louis, and Martha Graham. Indeed it was with the Paul Taylor Dance Company in 1981 at a Gala performance in what remains a unique occasion, he danced for the first time with his countryman and fellow Kirov defector, Mikhail Baryshnikov. With hilarious results they danced in Taylor's comic-book picture of American history and life, *From Sea to Shining Sea.*

Paul Taylor rehearsing Nureyev and Mikhail Baryshnikov in *From Sea to Shining Sea* for a Gala performance, April 1981, New York. Photograph by Lois Greenfield.

In class with Mikhail Baryshnikov, New York, 1977. Photograph Erik Dzenis.

With Erik Bruhn, presenter of the *Dance Magazine Award* to Nureyev, New York, 1973.
Photograph by Louis Péres.

Madame Jacques Chirac presenting the City's *Grande Medaille de Vermeil* to Rudolf Nureyev, on behalf of her husband, the Mayor of Paris, December 7, 1978. To the right is Pierre Bos, the Deputy Mayor of Paris. Photograph by J.C. Francolon/Gamma.

Nureyev after receiving an honorary doctorate from the Philadelphia College of the Performing Arts, April, 1980. Photograph by Wide World Photos.

228

229

The company he himself will run is almost certainly to be classically based, large, and of national proportions if not of national status. Insight, knowledge, concern, loyalty—these are all qualities that should enable him to be unusually well equipped to take over a company. For a time, perhaps, that very celebrity that has assisted his career as a dancer might tell against him, but one quality of Nureyev's that must never be overlooked or discounted is his plain and simple common sense, as well as his feel—always salutary—for the ridiculous and his nose for the pretentious.

As an artistic director, Nureyev would bring the whole breadth of his wide culture, and the curiosity that has stood him in such good stead as a dancer would be even more useful once he had his own company. He has always cultivated artists from other fields whether they be painters, sculptors, film directors, and all of this wide interest in the general cultural world would make him a rather different kind of director from the run of the mill dancer who finds himself acting almost as a ballet master in charge of a company instead of an artistic director in command of its cultural progress.

The kind of artistic director Nureyev would make can be fairly well postulated from his past record. Obviously his repertory would be based in part on the nineteenth century classics, but just as certainly those nineteenth century classics would be very much updated. Nureyev is always searching for new bottles for old wine. He is never content with the past.

Anyway, as a choreographer, that is what I said, the question is construction, and in a way, in modern terms, in contemporary terms, still without destroying the bone structure of the original creation. I mean the scholar and the dancer, in terms of scholar he holds these productions intact. . .

One of the things that first appalled him when he joined Britain's Royal Ballet was the fact that the British authorities and direction were intent, so far as possible, to maintain the old nineteenth century classics in their Russian forms in a way that they were not maintained even in Russia. This puzzled Nureyev more than almost anything else when he came to the West. He could see no more sense in this than he could see in trying to reproduce a Shakespearian production in the manner of Shakespeare's own time. He could see such a venture as possibly a legitimate experiment, but he could not see it as a normal way of maintaining the classics. In brief, Nureyev accepted the Soviet concept of productions that would place the choreographer Petipa, Ivanov, Gorsky, whoever—in much the same situation as the director of a classic play, while in the case of choreographers one would wish to keep certain key passages: The Kingdom of the Shades scene from *La Bayadère,* the Rose Adagio from *The Sleeping Beauty,* and certainly much of Ivanov's second act from *Swan Lake.* The rest, one would restore and renew and, in effect, re-choreograph.

This is not the place to enter an argument as to the rights and wrongs of choreographic fidelity for the nineteenth century ballet. Personally, I feel that there is a very strong case to be made for the attitude of both the Royal Ballet and American Ballet Theatre—at least in its pre-Baryshnikov days—that has taken the line that fidelity is the touchstone of survival, and that we should take choreography of the nineteenth century as seriously as we take choreography of the twentieth century.

No one pretends that *Les Sylphides,* in all its various guises and forms, is an identical reproduction of the Fokine original. And yet the intent to be as accurate as possible is very evident in every production of *Les Sylphides* that we know. Certainly after the days of Fokine, the attempts to maintain the choreographer's original vision are totally accepted— for that matter they are accepted by Nureyev. Nureyev would never dream of interfering with a ballet created in the twentieth century—for him it is only the nineteenth century classics that are fair game. From Michel Fokine onward, from the Diaghilev period in fact, Nureyev regards choreography as sacrosanct. This became an act of faith with Nureyev.

So we would expect this postulated Nureyev company to be based on the major classics, which would imply a company of at least seventy dancers.

The company of the London Festival Ballet celebrates Nureyev's twentieth anniversary in the West, after a performance of *Giselle* at the Coliseum, June 17, 1981. Photograph by Enid Theobald.

Whether Nureyev would act as his own choreographer, whether he would act more in a Diaghilev fashion, bringing collaborators together from across the world, this must remain to be seen. However, one cannot imagine a company that had the Nureyev imprint that was not extraordinarily alive to the trends and currents of contemporary thought. He is a man who lives very much in the present. He is never a person to look back. Even his attitude towards classics is one of revivifying, rather than resuscitating. He is a man at times almost obsessed with the new, and in this extent he does have a considerable degree in common with those two other great Russian animators of the dance in this century, Serge Diaghilev and George Balanchine, who both in totally different ways saw dance as an ongoing tide to be taken at the instant rather than a history of past steps or the memory of past attitudes.

Another quality that Nureyev would undoubtedly bring to the direction of a company is a very shrewd business sense, which you can call commercialism if you like, but which can never be denied. He has something of Sol Hurok's old touch of being able to gauge what the public wants, whether what it wants is in a performance or whether what it wants is in a programming. He has already been extensively responsible for the entirely new concept of dance packaging which has come to be called *Nureyev and Friends.* This idea developed with his manager, Sandor Gorlinsky, was worked out with his impresarios Sol Hurok and James H. Nederlander in America, and Victor Hochhauser, in London. Although the business arrangements were left to the impresarios, there was no doubt that the ideas, the programming, and the entire concept was Nureyev's. The concept has been quite remarkably original, not least when he produced a Diaghilev program in association with the Joffrey Ballet, later recorded for television on *Dance in America* for PBS. In 1982 this program won a George Foster Peabody Broadcasting Award for excellence in broadcasting.

Also, to market these programs, he has on several occasions left the traditional opera houses and moved into straight-forward Broadway houses. In this, he has followed the approach of such dancers in the past as Anna Pavlova and Mikhail Mordkin.

What the man has given already to dance is formidable—but this easily could be simply a preparation for what he is about to give. He is still a young man, full of knowledge, full of hope, and full of a special understanding of what dance and theater are all about.

The real Nureyev is the one people tend to forget—Nureyev the catalyst, Nureyev the impact, Nureyev the impulse, Nureyev the influence. Few men have left an impression so deep and so indelible on dance as that already left by Western ballet's strange but now much beloved Tatar visitor—a visitor who has stayed, become one of us, and made most of us one of his.

ANOTHER YEAR OF
GREATNESS FOR
RUDOLF
NUREYEV
HAPPY 41ST BIRTHDAY
FROM THE BIG APPLE

REPERTOIRE

NUREYEV'S REPERTOIRE IN RUSSIA

La Bayadère, full-length—Marius Petipa

Chopiniana, pas de deux—Michel Fokine

Le Corsaire, pas de deux—Marius Petipa/Vakhtang Chabukiani

Diana and Acteon, Solo and pas de deux—Jules Perrot/Vakhtang Chabukiani

Don Quixote—Marius Petipa

Flames of Paris, pas de deux—Vassily Vainonèn

The Fountain of Bakhchisarai, solo—Rostislav Zakharov

Gayané, Kurdish dance—Nina Anisimova

Giselle—Marius Petipa after Jean Coralli and Jules Perrot

Laurencia—Vakhtang Chabukiani

Legend of Love (dress rehearsal)—Yuri Grigorovich

Moskovsky Waltz—Vassily Vainonen

The Nutcracker—Vassily Vainonen

Pas de Quatre—Alexander Pushkin

Raymonda, pas de quatre—Marius Petipa

The Red Poppy, pas de quatre—Alexei Andreyev

★ Rosenkavalier Waltz—Leonid Jacobson

The Sleeping Beauty (The Prince and the Bluebird)—Marius Petipa

Swan Lake—Marius Petipa and Lev Ivanov

Taras Bulba, cossack scene—Boris Fenster

★ Valse Volante—Leonid Jacobson

NUREYEV'S REPERTOIRE IN THE WEST

This list includes only major productions of the classics. It is impractical, if not impossible, to catalog all the versions in which Nureyev has danced. Two examples: In addition to the original by Petipa and Ivanov, and his own, Nureyev has danced *Swan Lake* in productions by Frederick Ashton and Ninette de Valois, Vladimir Bourmeister, Erik Bruhn, John Cranko, John Field, Violette Verdy and Bruce Wells, among others; in *La Fille Mal Gardeé* Nureyev has danced versions provided by Frederick Ashton, Bronislava Nijinska, and Joseph Lazzini.

★ About a Dark House—Rudi van Dantzig

Adagio Hammerklavier—Hans van Manen

Adam and Eve (adapted for TV)—Birgit Cullberg

Afternoon of a Faun—Jerome Robbins

Agon—George Balanchine

Amazon Forest, pas de deux—Frederick Ashton

Antigone—John Cranko

Apollo—George Balanchine

L'Après-midi d'un Faune—Vaslav Nijinsky

Appalachian Spring—Martha Graham

Apparitions, ballroom scene—Frederick Ashton

Aureole—Paul Taylor

★ Bach Fantasia in C Minor—Kenneth MacMillan

• La Bayadère, Kingdom of the Shades—Marius Petipa/Rudolf Nureyev

Bayaderka, Act 4—Marius Petipa/Eugen Valukin

★ Big Bertha (adapted for TV)—Paul Taylor

Birthday Offering—Frederick Ashton

★ Choreographed on Nureyev
• Nureyev production

★ Blown by a Gentle Wind—Rudi van Dantzig

Book of Beasts—Paul Taylor

★ Le Bourgeois Gentilhomme—George Balanchine

★ The Canarsie Venus—Murray Louis

Checkmate—Ninette de Valois

Clytemnestra—Martha Graham

Conservatoire—August Bournonville

Coppélia—Erik Bruhn after Hans Beck and Harald Lander

• Le Corsaire, pas de deux—Rudolf Nureyev after Marius Petipa

★ Dances at a Gathering, as choreographed and staged for the Royal Ballet—Jerome Robbins

• Diana and Acteon, pas de deux—Rudolf Nureyev after Jules Perrot/Vakkhtang Chabukiani

Diversions—Kenneth MacMillan

★ Divertimento—Kenneth MacMillan

Don Juan—John Neumeier

Don Quixote, pas de deux—Marius Petipa

• Don Quixote—Rudolf Nureyev after Marius Petipa

The Dream—Frederick Ashton

★ Extase—Roland Petit

Ecuatorial—Martha Graham

★ Fantaisie—Erik Bruhn

★ Faun—Toer van Schayk

Field Figures—Glen Tetley

La Fille Mal Gardée—Frederick Ashton

Five Tangos—Hans van Manen

Flower Festival at Genzano, pas de deux—August Bournonville

233

Four Last Songs—Rudi van Dantzig
Four Schumann Pieces—Han van Manen
From Sea to Shining Sea—Paul Taylor
• Gayané, pas de deux—Nina Anisimova/Rudolf Nureyev
Giselle—Marius Petipa after Jean Coralli and Jules Perrot
Grand Pas Classique—Victor Gsovsky
Hamlet—Robert Helpmann
★ Hamlet Prelude (Hamlet and Ophelia)—Frederick Ashton
The Idiot—Valery Panov
★ Images of Love—Kenneth MacMillan
★ Jazz Calendar—Frederick Ashton
★ Le Jeune Homme et la Mort (adapted for TV)—Roland Petit
★ Laborintus—Glen Tetley
• Laurencia, pas de six—Vakhtang Chabukiani, staged by Rudolf Nureyev
The Lesson—Flemming Flindt
★ Lucifer—Martha Graham
• Manfred—Rudolf Nureyev
Manon—Kenneth MacMillan
★ Marco Spada—Pierre Lacotte after Joseph Mazilier
★ Marguerite and Armand—Frederick Ashton
The Merry Widow—Ruth Page
Miss Julie—Birgit Cullberg
★ Moment—Murray Louis
Monument to a Dead Boy—Rudi van Dantzig
The Moor's Pavane—José Limón
Night Journey—Martha Graham
• The Nutcracker—Rudolf Nureyev after Vassily Vainonen
• Paquita, pas de deux—Rudolf Nureyev after Marius Petipa
★ Paradise Lost—Roland Petit
★ Pelléas et Mélisande—Roland Petit
El Penitente—Martha Graham
Petrushka—Michel Fokine
Pierrot Lunaire—Glen Tetley
★ Poéme Tragique—Frederick Ashton

★ Choreographed on Nureyev
• Nureyev production

Prince Igor (Polovetsian Dances)—Michel Fokine
★ Prince Igor (Polovetsian Dances)—Ruth Page after Michel Fokine
The Prodigal Son—George Balanchine
• Raymonda, pas de quatre—Marius Petipa/Rudolf Nureyev
• Raymonda, dances from Act 3—Marius Petipa/Rudolf Nureyev
• Raymonda—Rudolf Nureyev after Marius Petipa
Les Rendezvous—Frederick Ashton
Romeo and Juliet—Kenneth MacMillan
• Romeo and Juliet—Rudolf Nureyev
★ The Ropes of Time—Rudi van Dantzig
Rubies—George Balanchine
Le Sacre du Printemps—Maurice Béjart
★ The Scarlet Letter—Martha Graham
Schéhérazade—Michel Fokine
★ Sideshow—Kenneth MacMillan
The Sleeping Beauty (Prince and Bluebird)—Marius Petipa
• The Sleeping Beauty—Rudolf Nureyev after Marius Petipa
Sonate à Trois—Maurice Béjart
Song of the Earth—Kenneth MacMillan
★ Songs of a Wayfarer—Maurice Béjart
★ Songs without Words—Hans van Manen
Le Spectre de la Rose—Michel Fokine
Swan Lake—Marius Petipa and Lev Ivanov
• Swan Lake—Rudolf Nureyev after Marius Petipa and Lev Ivanov
La Sylphide—Erik Bruhn after August Bournonville
La Sylphide—Pierre Lacotte after Filippo Taglioni
Les Sylphides—Michel Fokine
Symphonic Variations—Frederick Ashton
• Tancredi—Rudolf Nureyev
Theme and Variations—George Balanchine
Toccato and Fugue—Erik Bruhn
Toreador, pas de deux—Flemming Flindt after August Bournonville
★ Tristan—Glen Tetley
★ Ulysses—Rudi van Dantzig
La Ventana, pas de trois—August Bournonville/Erik Bruhn
★ Vivace—Murray Louis

NUREYEV'S ORIGINAL CHOREOGRAPHY

Manfred, full-length ballet
  Paris Opéra Ballet 1979
  Zurich Opera Ballet 1981
Romeo and Juliet, full-length ballet
  London Festival Ballet 1977
  La Scala Opera Ballet 1980
Swan Lake, solo for the Prince

Royal Ballet 1962
polonaise and mazurka
Royal Ballet 1963
Tancredi, full-length ballet
  Vienna State Opera Ballet 1966
The Tempest, full-length ballet
  Royal Ballet, to premiere December 2nd, 1982

REPERTOIRE

NUREYEV'S PRODUCTIONS OF THE CLASSICS

La Bayadère Kingdom of the Shades—Marius Petipa/
Rudolf Nureyev
    Royal Ballet 1963
    Paris Opéra Ballet 1974

Le Corsaire, pas de deux—Marius Petipa/Rudolf Nureyev
    Bell Telephone Hour 1962
    American Ballet Theatre 1962
    Chicago Opera Ballet 1962
    Royal Ballet 1962

Diana and Acteon, pas de deux—Jules Perrot/Vakhtang
Chabukiani/Rudolf Nureyev
    Bell Telephone Hour 1963
    Royal Academy of Dance Gala 1963
    American Ballet Theatre 1973

Don Quixote, full-length ballet—Rudolf Nureyev after
Marius Petipa
    Vienna State Opera Ballet 1966
    Australian Ballet 1970
    Marseille Opéra Ballet 1971
    Revised for Australian Ballet and for a film 1972
    Revived for Vienna State Opera Ballet 1977
    Zurich Opera Ballet 1980
    Norwegian Ballet 1981
    Paris Opéra Ballet 1981
    Boston Ballet 1982

Gayané, pas de deux—Nina Anisimova/Rudolf Nureyev
    Royal Academy of Dance Gala 1962

Laurencia, pas de six — Vakhtang Chabukiani/Rudolf
Nureyev
    Golden Hour Television, London 1964
    Royal Ballet 1965
    Revived for the Royal Ballet Touring Company 1972

The Nutcracker—Rudolf Nureyev after Vassili Vainonen
    pas de deux, Act 2
        Cannes 1962
    full-length ballet
        Royal Swedish Ballet 1967

    Royal Ballet 1968
    La Scala Opera Ballet 1969
    Ballet of Teatro Colón, Buenos Aires 1971
    Revised for Royal Ballet 1973
    Berlin Opera Ballet 1979

Paquita, grand pas—Marius Petipa/Rudolf Nureyev
    Royal Academy of Dance Gala, 1964
    Revived by Marika Besobrazova for La Scala Opera
        Ballet 1970
    Vienna State Opera Ballet 1971
    American Ballet Theatre 1971

Raymonda—Marius Petipa/Rudolf Nureyev
    pas de quatre
        Quartet 1962
    dances from Act 3
        Fonteyn and Nureyev Tour 1963

Raymonda—Rudolf Nureyev after Marius Petipa
    full-length ballet
        Royal Ballet Touring Company 1964
        Australian Ballet 1965
        Zurich Opera Ballet 1972
        American Ballet Theatre 1975

Raymonda, Act 3—Rudolf Nureyev after Marius Petipa
    Royal Ballet Touring Company 1966
    Norwegian Ballet 1968
    Royal Ballet 1969

The Sleeping Beauty—Rudolf Nureyev after Marius Petipa
    solo, Act 3
        Royal Ballet 1962
    full-length ballet
        La Scala Opera Ballet 1966
        National Ballet of Canada 1972
        London Festival Ballet 1975
        Vienna State Opera Ballet 1981

Swan Lake, full-length ballet — Rudolf Nureyev after
Marius Petipa and Lev Ivanov
    Vienna State Opera Ballet 1964

NUREYEV AND FRIENDS

In cooperation with his impresarios Sol Hurok and James H. Nederlander in New York and Sandor A. Gorlinsky and Victor Hochhauser in London, Rudolf Nureyev has independently presented a series of programs in various Broadway theaters in New York and in the Coliseum in London beginning in 1974 and continuing through the present. Nureyev has danced in every performance in almost every ballet. Similar programs have been presented in Paris, Washington, D.C., and elsewhere.

Works by Frederick Ashton, George Balanchine, Maurice Béjart, Flemming Flindt, Martha Graham, José Limón, Murray Louis, Paul Taylor, Glen Tetley, Rudi van Dantzig, and Hans van Manen have been combined, especially in London, with the full-length classics, including Nureyev's own ballets: *Don Quixote, Manfred, Romeo and Juliet,* and *The Sleeping Beauty.* Major ballet companies, including the Boston Ballet, Dutch National Ballet, the Joffrey Ballet, London Festival Ballet, National Ballet of Canada, Scottish Ballet, Zurich Opera Ballet have joined him in those ballets as well as in *Coppélia, Giselle, Swan Lake, La Sylphide,* and *Les Sylphides.* In the last named, Margot Fonteyn, Natalia Makarova and Lynn Seymour danced together for the first time anywhere.

Ballets included are: About a Dark House, Amazon Forest, Apollo, L'après-midi d'un Faune, Aureole, Le Bourgeois Gentilhomme, Canarsie (Brighton) Venus, Clytemnestra, Conservatoire, Coppélia, Le Corsaire, Don Quixote, Ecuatorial, Faun, Flower Festival pas de deux, Four Schumann Pieces, Giselle, The Lesson, Lucifer, Manfred, Marguerite and Armand, Moment, The Moor's Pavane, Night Journey, Petrushka, Pierrot Lunaire, Romeo and Juliet, Rubies, Scarlet Letter, Schéhérazade, Sonate à Trois, Songs of a Wayfarer, The Sleeping Beauty, Le Spectre de la Rose, Swan Lake, La Sylphide, Les Sylphides, Toreador pas de deux, Vivace.

INDEX

Page numbers in italics indicate illustrations.

236